STEHEKIN

The Enchanted Valley

STEHEKIN

A Guide to
The Enchanted Valley

by Fred T. Darvill, Jr., M.D.

Signpost Books

STEHEKIN: The Enchanted Valley
© 1981 by Fred T. Darvill, Jr.

Published by
SIGNPOST BOOKS
8912 192nd SW
Edmonds, WA 98020

Edited by Mary Ann Cameron

Darvill, Fred T   1927-
    Stehekin, a guide to the enchanted valley.

    Bibliography: p. 106
    Includes index.
    1.   Hiking—Washington (State)—North Cascades National
Park—Guide-books.   2. Natural history—Washington (State)—
North Cascades National Park.   3. North Cascades National Park
—Guide-books.   I. Title.
GV199.42.W22N673   917.97'5'0443   80-16628
ISBN   0-913140-42-2

Preface

Appetite whetted by many viewings of "The Wilderness Alps of the Stehekin,"the author first arrived in the Valley on The Lady of the Lake June 19, 1964. Near the landing, a strong feeling of *deja vu* came over me. Although I had never been here before (in this life), I had a very strong strange feeling that I was coming home to a place that I knew well and treasured. Clearly, the Valley was enchanted! The "phantom deer" arose that evening on the walk from the landing to Rainbow Falls; the beauty and peace caused the cares of the outside more mundane world to fall away, leaving my soul pristine and pure. Somehow I knew deeper than knowing all else that I belonged in this Valley.

By the fall of 1964 I had purchased five acres of land; in April of 1965 the survey had been completed; in September 1967, the shell of an A-frame sat adjacent to a side channel of the Stehekin River. I have returned at least once a year since 1967, save in 1969 when the death of a very close person who also treasured the Valley made memories too poignant to brave a return until 1970. Over the past 15 years, I have walked most of the trails reachable from the Valley without crossing a road. I have also walked into the Valley up lake from Prince Creek, and via Cascade Pass, Bridge Creek, McAlester Pass, Rainbow Lake, and from Chelan on the Summit Trail.

As I write this on a grey wet day in December 1979, it is good to know that my small A-frame exists at this moment beside the Stehekin River, probably in the first snowfall of the season. It is a comfort to know that the enchanted valley is there!

Since 1976, I have been privileged to share my humble cabin with the former Ginny Turner. She, the Valley, and I are "sympatico." It is my pleasure to dedicate this book to my wife Ginny, and to share this most lovely place with those of you who read this publication.

Dr. F. T. Darvill

MAJOR RIVERS AND CREEKS

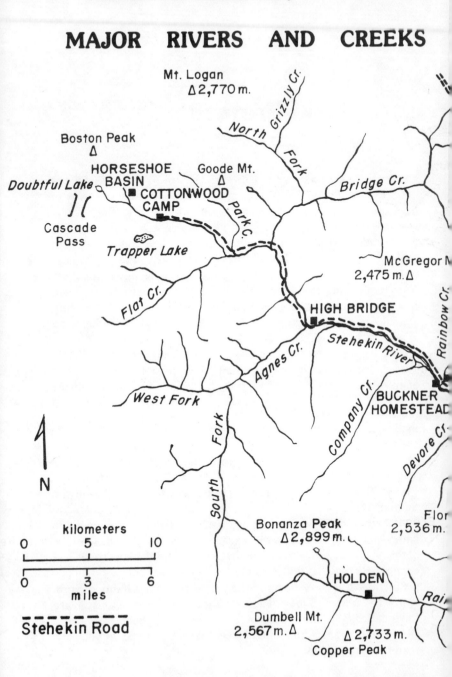

See pages 50—51 for map of *trails* of the Stehekin Valley

OF THE STEHEKIN VALLEY

North Cascades
Highway

Grizzly Cr.

North Fork

Bridge Cr.

McGregor Mt.
2,475 m. Δ

McAlester Mt.
Δ 2,416 m.

Rainbow Cr.

HIGH BRIDGE

Agnes Cr.

Stehekin River

Boulder Cr.

Lone Mt.
Δ 2,047 m.

Company Cr.

RAINBOW FALLS

BUCKNER
HOMESTEAD

Devore Cr.

STEHEKIN LANDING

Bonanza Peak
Δ 2,899 m.

Flora Mt.
2,536 m. Δ

Riddle Cr.

Fish Cr.

Finney Pea

Cascade C. Δ 2,4

HOLDEN

Railroad Cr.

LUCERNE

Prince Cr.

Dumbell Mt.
567 m. Δ

Δ 2,733 m.
Copper Peak

Domke
Lake

Contents

There is no opiate like alpine pedestrianism.
— Mark Twain

Introduction

Stehekin is a Northwest Indian word loosely translated as "the way through." The Indians no doubt gave it that name after discovering that the Valley provided a relatively easy route between the east and west sides of Washington. However, for present generations, it may represent a totally different "way through" than the physical trans-mountain passage it represented to early man.

Beset by inflation, energy shortages, burdensome taxation, the specter of atomic holocaust, noise, and the pressures inevitable in a finite world with an ever enlarging population, modern man has need of periodic re-creation in order to stay sane. At Stehekin, at least now, and hopefully indefinitely, it is possible to stop the world, and get off.....off to a fishing hole in an un- believably clear stream where trout rise to a skillfully presented fly.....off to green meadows where acres of flowers greet the sun, and welcome the frequent rains.....off to the summit of a high peak, a cathedral more splendid than any ever built by man where dialogue with the Divine seems easier.....off to be alone with beauty, and to heal; to regain the strength and the courage to again return to the real world where substantive dragons lurk, and the uglies and the horrors are too often *bona fide* rather than nightmares.

Shrangri-La is not in far off Nepal; it is located at the head of Lake Chelan. Here in this enchanted valley you too may find the way through!

Important Information

Data about the Stehekin area can be obtained from several offices of North Cascades National Park (800 State Street, Sedro Woolley, WA 98284 [206/855-1331] *OR* P.O. Box 549, Chelan, WA 98816 [509/682-2540] *OR* Stehekin, WA 98852).

Information about the surrounding National Forests, including the Glacier Peak Wilderness Area, can be obtained from Mount Baker-Snoqualmie National Forest (1022 1st Avenue, Seattle, WA 98104 (206) 442-5400); Wenatchee National Forest (301 Yakima Street, P.O. Box 811, Wenatchee, WA 98801 (509) 662-4335); and Okanogan National Forest (Box 950, Okanogan, WA 98840 (509) 422-2704).

The best overall map of the area is the 1:100,000 topographic map (metric contour lines) of the North Cascades National Park and the Chelan and Ross Lake National Recreation Areas, published by the U.S. Geological Survey, Branch of Distribution, Box 25286, Denver Federal Center, Denver, CO 80225 ($2). Other topographic maps providing greater local detail can be obtained from the USGS. A topographic map of the Glacier Peak Wilderness Area is available from the Mt. Baker-Snoqualmie and Wenatchee National Forests, and is particularly recommended. An alternative to the USGS maps are the Green Trails maps, which are more up-to-date concerning roads and trails than are the USGS maps. Green Trails maps cover the area in 15' segments, while the USGS maps are in the 7½' series. USGS maps are more detailed, but four USGS maps are needed to cover the area included in one Green Trails map. See specific trail description for names of appropriate maps. An index of maps is on pages 106-7. Other non-topographic maps can be obtained from both Forest and Park Service offices.

The Park Service has published an expanded topographic map titled *Main Trails and Back Country Camps, North Cascades Complex, Washington* (1980). This map shows all elevations in meters. All designated campsites are shown. Fires are allowed at campsites marked in red; fires are prohibited at sites marked in green. There is also designation of campsites for horses and for boaters. The route of the Pacific Crest Trail also is shown on this map. Review is strongly suggested when planning trips in the Stehekin area.

For information about transportation, contact the Lake Chelan Boat Company, P.O. Box 186, Chelan, WA (509/682-2224). For

Lady of the Lake arriving at Stehekin

air transport from Chelan to Stehekin, contact Chelan Airways, Chelan, WA 98816 (509/682-5555). For accommodations at Stehekin, contact the North Cascades Lodge, Stehekin, WA 98852. Phone contact is uncertain, but sometimes the lodge can be reached at 509/662-3822. For information on horseback and pack trips, contact the Cascade Corrals (Ray Courtney), Stehekin, WA 98852; there is no phone. For climbing information about specific peaks, research the involved mountain in the "Cascade Alpine Guide" by Fred Beckey (published by The Mountaineers in 1977).

History

Prior to the coming of the white man, Indians were familiar with the Stehekin Valley. Marred pictographs, located just above the present high water level of Lake Chelan, can still be seen near Stehekin. Little is known about the ancient Indian artists who painted these strange red figures.

According to U.S. Army reports a hundred years ago, local Indian tribes also considered them a puzzle. Colonel Merriam, in 1880 the commanding officer of Army troops stationed in Chelan, reported the pictographs at the head of the lake. But he stated that the present Chelan Indians could tell nothing about them except that they must have been made by people who lived there long before the Chelans had come to the area. In addition, early explorers reported the presence of Indian trails in the Skehekin Valley, and Indian canoes, presumably kept there for travel down the lake, were found at the head of Lake Chelan by prospectors in 1877. No Indian tribe permanently inhabited the Stehekin area, however.

The first white man in the Stehekin area was probably Alexander Ross of the British Northwest Company, in charge of Ft. Okanogan, a fur trading post erected in 1811. In 1814, he traveled up the Methow River, and crossed Twisp Pass, entering what is now the North Cascades National Park. At the present site of Fireweed, he probably turned left, down Bridge Creek to the Stehekin River, then went west, crossing over Cascade Pass and down the Cascade River toward the Skagit. Less likely, he turned right at Fireweed, crossed Rainy Pass and followed Granite and Ruby Creeks toward the Skagit River. Apparently he was the first white man to cross the North Cascades, using Indian guides to lead him over primitive trails. Unfortunately, the Indians deserted him and he had to retrace his steps before reaching Puget Sound. Although he did not proceed down the valley to the head of the lake, his feat of being the first white man to cross the Cascade crest has earned him a permanent place in North Cascades history.

In the early 1880s, white men began to explore the Stehekin Valley. In 1882, a U.S. Army expedition under the command of Lt. Henry Pierce left Ft. Colville on August 1, 1882 and proceeded west, up the Methow to the Twisp River, then up to War Creek. He followed that valley to what is presently War Creek Pass and crossed the Juanita Lake meadow to a point where he could see the head of Lake Chelan, presumably at Purple Pass (or perhaps Boulder Butte).

He stated: "As I gazed westward from a height of 6,500 feet above the sea and 5,800 feet above the lake, a scene of remarkable grandeur was presented. To the south and west were the rugged peaks of the Cascade Mountains covered with everlasting snow. At our feet, reposed (Lake) Chelan in color like an artificial lake of thick plate glass, while the Stehekin River brought its clay-tinted waters with many a winding down the narrow canyon that opened to the North.'' After accomplishing the difficult descent to the lake, Pierce described the valley bottom as a ''dense jungle of cottonwood, willows, firs, and underbrush with frequent lagoons covered by almost tropical growth of rush grass, ferns, and other marshy vegetation.''

Proceeding up the valley on a ''most imperfect trail'', Pierce noticed at the time the party forded Bridge Creek there was a crude bridge of drift logs, presumably used by Indians for crossing the creek. The group crossed Cascade Pass on August 27. Near the mouth of the Cascade River, an Indian summer lodge was located. By September 1, the patrol had pushed west to a point near the present town of Sedro Woolley. The account of this exploration was published by the Federal Government in 1883.

Mining activity brought the first permanent white settlers into the Stehekin Valley. Although a Mr. McKee may have prospected the area as early as 1875, brothers George and John Rouse made the first major ore discovery in 1886 on the edge of Doubtful Lake. Gold, silver, and lead were found. Multiple other claims were staked shortly thereafter, particularly in the Horseshoe Basin area.

There also were claims on the North Fork of Bridge Creek. Mining activity was substantial and vigorous in the 1890s with many active claims at the head of the Stehekin Valley. To supply the mines, a road was constructed from the lakeshore which eventually reached Horseshoe Basin. The original road went up the hillside above the current site of High Bridge and can still be followed to this day. The road was actually passable by cars as late as 1948, when some of the mines in Horseshoe Basin, particularly the Black Warrior, were still being worked. (Erosion and overgrowth have closed the road between Cottonwood and Horseshoe Basin now.) The ore never proved to be high grade. The difficulties of conveying the ore from mine to railroad in conjunction with the short working season (considering the amount of snowfall at high elevations) made the mines economically unfeasible, and none are presently in operation.

Although in 1980 only one 21-acre claim remains in private ownership, there still is a substantial amount of abandoned mining equipment and debris in the Horseshoe Basin area. History buffs can imagine the courage and fortitude required to locate and work these ''glory holes'', particularly if one wintered over as was done in 1909. A tunnel through the snow connected the sleeping cabin with the mine entrance. The Black Warrior Mine is listed on the National Register of Historic Places. It was checked by the NPS in

1979 and is considered safe to enter.

Rouse's mining camp stood approximately at the present site of the Basin Creek Campground. Pieces of this structure and abandoned equipment still can be found in the area today.

At the junction of Bridge Creek and the Stehekin, a substantial community existed in 1892 to supply the mines; this community was still active in 1904. Presently several cabins, the ruins of a sawmill, and the debris of several other structures can be found in and around the Bridge Creek area. Other camps and cabins were located up Bridge Creek and further up the Stehekin. There were two cabins and a sawmill at one time at Doubtful Lake. Most of these early structures have long since collapsed under the weight of the heavy winter snows.

The mining frontier in Stehekin created an immediate need for transportation services. Those services emerged in two ways; steamboats on Lake Chelan and road construction within the Valley developed in the 1890s.

The first steamer on Lake Chelan was called The Belle and made its appearance on the Lake in 1889. The Stehekin, the largest steamer at the time on Lake Chelan at 100 feet long with a 16 foot beam, was commissioned in 1893 and retired in 1904. In August 1900, the first Lady of the Lake was launched. This boat was 112 feet in length with a 16 foot beam. There has been an active Lady of the Lake on Lake Chelan since that date. The original boats were cord wood burning steamboats; petroleum powered engines did not appear until about 1914.

The Speedway was built on the lake and was functional when the Lake Chelan Boat Company was incorporated in 1929. The still-operational Lady of the Lake was built on the coast and served as a tour boat on Lake Roosevelt before she was moved to Lake Chelan in 1945. The currently operating Lady II was built by the Lake Chelan Boat Company in the early 1970s and went into regular service in June 1976. She is licensed to carry 350 passengers.

Fuel, vehicles, building materials, and all goods either too large or too heavy to go on the regular passenger boat are transported on the freight barge, the Allen Stone. During the summer, the barge makes a regular weekly trip up lake.

Overall, the steamboat era on Lake Chelan provided miners, homesteaders, and tourists with adequate service for many years, and it was one of the most colorful chapters in Stehekin's history.

In 1896, work began on the "Cascade Wagon Road" west of Cascade Pass and continued fitfully for many years. Although shown on some maps in the past, the road was never developed to the point where any vehicle could follow the road to, much less over, the crest of the Cascades. Although a "mine to market" road was constructed in 1948 from east of Marblemount to within two miles west of the crest of Cascade Pass, no connection was ever built between this road and the Horseshoe Basin Road.

Excluding the crude and often steep access to the mines in the upper Stehekin Valley, road-building never went much beyond the 23 miles which exist today. Nevertheless, over a half century or so, several plans to link the Valley with the outside were pursued with some seriousness. Even railroad interests considered building a railroad over Cascade Pass. The Stehekin Valley and the pass were surveyed in the course of evaluating routes for railroads, but eventually such plans were abandoned in favor of a route over Stevens Pass. The Cascade Pass route always "lucked out"and fortunately it remains pristine today insofar as automotive and railroad traffic is concerned.

The mineral discoveries in the late 1880s also attracted homesteaders to the lower Stehekin Valley. Several of the first settlers were prospectors; others were engaged in supplying the men at the mines in the back country. Among the earliest settlers were miner J. W. Horton; hotelman George Hall; prospector Dan Devore; miner and homesteader Bill Buzzard; M. E. Field, hotel proprietor; F. F. Keller, prospector; and the W. F. Purple family (after whom Purple Point, Purple Creek, and Purple Pass were named), who arrived in the area in 1892.

Mr. Field first operated a smaller hotel, the Argonault, which was in operation in 1892. In 1900, Field began construction of a new hotel, which was opened in July, and was known thereafter as the Hotel Field. This wilderness inn was later enlarged, and by

Field Hotel as seen from the cliffs above Purples (i.e., above the present Stehekin Landing)

Field Hotel, with McGregor Mountain in background

1910 had developed into an elaborate building of three stories; its 50 rooms could accommodate 100 guests. Indeed it was one of the most well-known hotels in the Pacific Northwest. In those days, everyone who came up the lake had to stay overnight since the boats were unable to make the round trip in one day. Later commonly remembered as the Field Hotel, the building served as the focus of valley activities for almost two decades.

The hotel was demolished in 1927, shortly before the Chelan Dam raised the water in the lake to a sufficient height to flood the hotel site. The present Golden West Lodge, currently being used as an interpretative site by the Park Service, was partially built out of the material removed from the Field Hotel. The Golden West Hotel operated for 44 years (1927-1971), the longest continuous operation in Stehekin's history.

In the early 1900s, another lodging place was started on the site of the present Stehekin. This inn, known as the Purple House (named after its owner), was less plush than the Field Hotel; both were in operation in 1910. In 1927, the small store and post office were also moved from the head of the lake to their present location.

Curt Courtney, brother of Ray Courtney, operated lodging and restaurant facilities at Stehekin for a number of years prior to the transfer of land management responsibility from the Forest Service to the Park Service in 1968. Shortly thereafter, the buildings at Stehekin were acquired by the federal government, renovated and remodeled, and are presently leased to concessioners to operate. There have been several operators of the North Cascades Lodge over the past twelve years, including long-time Stehekin resident Robert Byrd, and the present

Stehekin School, now a historical place

concessioner Gary Gibson, son of Ernie Gibson who has piloted the float plane between Chelan and Stehekin since the end of World War II.

By 1892, there were enough children at Stehekin to justify the establishment of a school. A number of structures were used temporarily. The oldest known school building still standing is the Kronk Cabin (named after an early Chelan County commissioner) about five miles up the valley from the lake. In 1921, the citizens of the Valley and the U. S. Forest Service reached an agreement to erect a permanent school house. The parents contributed their time and skill, and the current Stehekin School, originally one room built of logs, was established on Forest Service land a few yards from spectacular Rainbow Falls. Although a bit larger presently, for a long time it was the last one room school still in use in Washington.

Other historical buildings include the Buckner Cabin, originally constructed by William Buzzard in 1889. The Buckner Ranch can currently be toured with a Park Service guide.

Bill Buzzard and Henry Buckner were two of the many prospectors reaching the Stehekin Valley in the late 1800s. The current Buckner Ranch was originally a homestead of 160 acres, first claimed by Bill Buzzard around 1900. Henry Buckner, after whom Buckner Peak was named, had a younger brother, William Van, who came to the valley and eventually bought the current

Buckner Ranch from Bill Buzzard. Van's son, Harry, came to the ranch in 1911, at the age of 16, and never left the valley for any significant period of time thereafter except to serve in the Army in World War I. His father turned the ranch over to Harry in 1918, and Harry Buckner was a Stehekin institution by the 1960s when the author first reached the Valley. At that time, he was continuing to operate his ranch, which obtained irrigation water via a wooden pipe from Boulder Creek. He also was the Stehekin postmaster until his death in the late 1970s.

The Courtney Cabin on the west side of the river above Company Creek is still standing. There is no public transportation to this location, and no on-site interpretation. In 1917, a fish hatchery was built near Rainbow Falls. When it was abandoned by the State, it was converted into a community hall for the residents of Stehekin.

Although much has changed in the Stehekin Valley since the pioneering days, there still remains much evidence that the "old way of life" has not disappeared. Several current residents of the Valley have lived there all their lives, including Ray Courtney, perhaps the last of the true "mountain men". This man probably knows the Stehekin area better than anyone; the Courtneys understand and accept the traditional lifestyle of this isolated valley. Ray and his wife, Esther, still make a living in the Valley by doing packing for sightseers, hikers, hunters, and photographers.

Other names, such as Welsey, Imus, Bergman, Byrd, and Fellows are additional examples of Stehekin's link with the past.

FIRE LOOKOUTS

In the early 1930s, the U. S. Forest Service constructed an extensive number of fire lookout houses throughout the North Cascades. In those days, some of the locations were really remote, taking two days to reach. The personnel manning the lookout stations were generally unusual people, self sufficient and able to tolerate prolonged solitude. Communication initially was by heliograph or telephone; lines had to be restrung yearly since winter treefall invariably made the system nonfunctional until repairs were made. Later, two-way radio was utilized, mostly for reporting fires, but in the evening, the "lookout's hour" allowed 30 minutes of personal communication to diminish loneliness. In the center of each structure was a range finder, an instrument for precisely locating a fire. When not fire watching, the lookouts fetched water, maintained the lookout structures, did trail work and cursed the insects.

Artist's impression of the McGregor fire lookout house as viewed from an airplane in 1940s; Stehekin Valley in background

As aircraft became more reliable and less expensive to operate, aerial fire patrol flights were thought to be cheaper and more efficient. Gradually, the lookouts were phased out. The buildings were declared to be no longer useful and were burned. Many currently existing pathways to highpoints originally were constructed to build and supply the fire lookout system. (A few lookouts in the North Cascades still exist, and are manned; an even smaller number have been leased to outdoor clubs, or are maintained by volunteers; however, none are located in the Stehekin area.)

There were several lookouts in the vicinity of the Stehekin Valley. McGregor Mountain was first utilized as a lookout site in 1918 or 1919. The lookout person lived in a small tent camp at the foot of the peak where the Park Service campsite is presently located. A 1,100 foot tramway was constructed in the early summer of 1923 to move materials from the horse camp to the summit; the lookout house was built later that summer. It was a 12 foot by 12 foot frame cupola cabin located on the very summit.

The tramway was not too practical as each year it had to be repaired and restrung due to damage from the ice and snow of winter. It was eventually abandoned and material from the horse camp was backpacked to the lookout.

Early communication was by heliograph from the lookout to the Stehekin Ranger Station. Eventually a telephone line, which ran from Stehekin to High Bridge, was extended to the lookout. This line was still in use when the station was abandoned in the late 1940s, although two-way radio had been instituted at about that time. The lookout was destroyed in 1953.

Thirty to forty gallons of kerosene were used each season for cooking, heating, and melting snow and ice from the Sandalee Glacier on the northeast side of the peak; snow and ice were the only available water supplies.

During lightning storms, the person in the lookout sat on a stool which had glass insulators on all four legs. All lookouts had lightning rods and conducting wires to ground electricity, since mountain peaks are high risk places for lightning to strike. At night during electrical storms, the metal on the station would sometimes glow with an eerie light due to the buildup of static electricty.

During World War II, the lookouts, including McGregor, also served as aircraft identification stations.

The Boulder Butte Lookout was a standard 12 x 12 foot ground base station built in 1938 or 1939. Building materials were packed in from the Twisp River Road on packhorses. There was telephone communication to Stehekin and Twisp. This lookout was destroyed in the early 1950s.

Stiletto Peak was manned for several seasons prior to 1931; the lookout person lived in a tent camp, and made his observations from the top of the mountain. In 1931, the standard 12 x 12 foot lookout house was packed in from the Twisp River Road and erected. There was telephone communication to both the Stehekin Ranger District via Bridge Creek and to the Twisp Ranger District. This lookout was destroyed in the late 1940s or early 1950s.

The lookout on Goode Ridge was built about 1933. The building material was packed from the Stehekin Road to a site on Goode Ridge overlooking Greenview Lake. It was a standard 12 x 12 foot house with the usual fire finder in the center of the building. Communication was by telephone to the Stehekin Ranger District. Winter storms smashed this structure, and the winds blew the debris over the edge of the ridge into the lake basin. It was rebuilt in 1934 and used for several seasons; it was burned by the Forest Service in the late 1940s or early 1950s.

Horton Butte Lookout was built in 1932 or 1933. The building was structurally the same as the other lookouts, but only 10 x 10 feet in size. It was packed in by horses from Lake Chelan up Fish Creek. The station was an emergency station, manned only during periods of high fire danger. It also was destroyed by the Forest Service in the early 1950s.

There was also a lookout on Domke Mountain. This was built on a 100-foot high steel tower with two log cabins at the base for support. All are long gone.

CREATION OF THE NATIONAL PARK

A national park in the North Cascades was first proposed at a campfire gathering of the Mazamas, Portland's famed mountaineering club, at high camp near Mt. Baker in 1906. By 1910, the Mt. Baker Club of Bellingham was vigorously promoting national park status for Mt. Baker; that proposal would probably have been enacted, but for the coming of World War I.

The dreamers would not give up. Other efforts to acquaint the nation with its incomparable northwest mountain wilderness were made, and by 1937 an investigating committee of the Department of the Interior had reported back that "the area is unquestionably of national park caliber, is more valuable used as such than for any other use now ascertainable, and should receive park status. . . it will outrank in its scenic, recreation and wildlife values any existing national park and any other possibility for such a park within the United States". Still it was passed over as another great war flamed in Europe.

The final successful effort began about 1956 with the organization of the North Cascades Conservation Council. This group spearheaded the 12 years of continuous effort required to create the North Cascades National Park and its associated recreational areas; assisting groups included the Sierra Club, the Seattle Mountaineers, the Federation of Western Outdoor Clubs, and its affiliated organizations within Washington. Many, many individuals contributed long years of unselfish effort; among those making outstanding contributions were Dr. Patrick Goldsworthy, Phillip Zaleskey, Polly Dyer, Dr. William Halliday, Mike McCloskey, Brock Evans, David Brower, Harvey Manning, and Charles Hessey.

A 16mm film produced by the Sierra Club and narrated by Dave Brower entitled "The Wilderness Alps of the Stehekin" was a major means of acquainting people with the unusual beauty and recreational potential of the Stehekin Valley.

U. S. Representative Thomas Pelly filed the initial bill for creation of the park in Congress. After some years of further effort, a joint study team sponsored by the Departments of

Agriculture and Interior evaluated the area and held public hearings.   A substantial book containing their findings and recommendations was published entitled "The North Cascades Study Report".   The bills to create the park and recreation area were filed in the Senate by Senator Henry M. Jackson, and in the House by Congressman Lloyd Meeds.   The final bill as adopted was a compromise between the conflicting interests of those desirous of preserving the area for its recreational and esthetic values, and of those concerned with extracting resources, particularly timber, from the area.   As a result of this compromise, many superior areas now have legal protection, but a number of equally fine locations are without any protection whatsoever.

After approximately 62 years of bubbling and simmering controversy, the issue was finally resolved on October 2, 1968 when President Lyndon Johnson signed the legislation transferring the land now in the park and two recreation areas from the Forest Service to the Park Service.

Following establishment of the park, the federal government purchased two-thirds of the available private land in the Stehekin Valley.   Roughly one-third of the private land, originally homesteaded, remains in private hands.   In 1979, county zoning regulations were being explored in an effort to prevent inappropriate use of the remaining valley lands in private hands while simultaneously allowing owners reasonable use of their property.

Rocks and Glaciers (Geology)

Rocks changed by pressure and heat when they were miles below the surface of the earth form the core of the North Cascades. Volcanic and sedimentary rocks, laid down in past geologic ages, mostly upon the sea floor, predominate on the flanks of the range. The crust of the earth now exposed in the mountains was strongly folded and broken by great fractures in the geologic past.   There also are large bodies of massive granite that formed underground, invading the earlier rocks.   The Cascades are recently uplifted mountains in terms of geologic time.   This uplift caused deep dissection by streams, followed by glacial erosion during the ice age.   Since the end of the ice age, erosion by glaciers has been restricted to higher altitudes; most of the current erosion is due to swift stream action.   The Skagit River cuts across the core of the range because it was able to erode downward as fast as the range was being elevated.

Mt. Baker (Koma Kulshan) at 10,778 feet and Glacier Peak at

10,528 feet are large dormant composite or stratovolcanoes, made up of alternating layers of lava and fragmental cinders and ash. These peaks are recent additions to the North Cascades geologic scene.

Mt. Baker erupted five times in the 19th century; the last eruption was in 1870. Steam and sulfur fumes still issue from the summit crater periodically.

Glacier Peak has not been active within historical times. About 12,000 years ago, it blasted pumice over the North Cascades from Lake Chelan to southern Alberta. There is no summit activity currently. Both mountains, however, have active hot springs scattered about their bases indicating that the "fires below" are not completely out.

Paradoxically, the greatest danger from the volcanoes, should they awaken, is not from lava but from floods and mud flows. The latter, mixtures of hot rock, debris and water from melted snow and ice, can travel up to 50 miles per hour, destroying everything in their path.

The dominant bedrock at the upper end of Lake Chelan is classified as pre-Jurassic metamorphic, and is called Skagit Gneiss (pronounced nice); in other words, the cliffs around Stehekin are over 180 million years old; the original rock has been slowly changed by powerful earth forces into the present coarse grained and banded rock.

Beginning about one million years ago, alpine glaciers periodically grew and descended the Stehekin Valley; at its longest, this glacier reached from Cascade Pass to the Columbia River. Lake Chelan lies in a classic example of the U-shaped glacial trough; stream-carved valleys by contrast are classically V-shaped. The glacial ice scoured and scooped downward deeply along much of the lake, and in places gouged 583 feet below sea level. The ice was approximately a mile deep at the time of its maximum advance. There is evidence that in places the depth of glacial excavation exceeded 2,000 feet; in other words, the preexisting valleys were cut down and deepened very substantially by the ice.

Geologists are still unsure how many times the alpine glaciers descended the valley; based on data obtained about ice advances elsewhere, it is felt that there were several advances, most probably four. Glacial striations, huge grooves in the rock of the valley floor cut by rocks moved along at the bottom of the glacial ice, are another clue confirming the glacial origin of the valley. Rounded valley bluffs also strongly suggest glacial sculpturing. Equally important are erratics; these are rocks totally different geologically from those of the area in which they are found, which could only have reached the area by being carried along on the top of glacial ice. Erratics were quarried by the glacier near its source

Round Mt.   Domke Mt.

The Chelan Glacier as seen from summit of McGregor Mtn. (at maximum depth, the ice covered both Round and Domke Mtns.)

and deposited along the sides of, or at the end of, the glacier as the ice receded.

When coming up the lake, notice 4,000 foot Domke Mountain on the west near Lucerne and 4,397 foot Round Mountain on the east. Both of these hills were smoothed and rounded by the ice of the Lake Chelan, Railroad Creek, and Fish Creek Glaciers as they joined together in this area.

The Chelan or Alpine Glacier had receded well up the lake to approximately 25 Mile Creek by the time of the furthest advance of lowland ice across the Columbia Plateau (the Continental Glacier). This glacier invaded the lower end of the already excavated valley, and blocked the exit of water. The lake level was raised hundreds of feet as a result. Eventually water spilled out of the lake into the Columbia River via the Knapp and Navarre Coolees.

The Continental Glacier had little erosive power when it filled the lower Chelan Valley. Evidence of this are the extensive series of terraces in the lower valley, which were formed stepwise as the glacier receded.   In addition, there are basalt (lava) erratics, locally known as haystack rocks, which are scattered over the lower valley; no such rock exists between Cascade Pass and the lower valley, so the rock had to be brought in from Central Washington rather than down the Stehekin Valley.

One cannot fail to be impressed while traveling on Lake Chelan with the power of the almost one mile thick ice sheet which created the trough.   Almost equally impressive is the power of running water.   The alluvial fan at the mouth of Prince Creek is an impressive monument to the flash flood.   Although there was a pre-existing flat area at the creek mouth before 1947, on which the Forest Service had located buildings, the creek outflow area was much smaller until a massive thunderstorm hit the Prince Creek drainage in 1947.   As a result, a wall of water came down Prince Creek, tumbling huge boulders and depositing them at the edge of the lake as you see them today.   The buildings in the path of the rocks and water were destroyed. It is somewhat frightening to realize that natural forces of this magnitude still occur in our present world.

Life Zones

The type of vegetation and, to some degree, the animal inhabitants of an area depend upon altitude and somewhat on amount of precipitation (snow and rain).   Life zones are also related to the relative distance of the area between the equator and the North Pole.

In the Stehekin area, four life zones are encountered between lakeshore and mountaintop.

The yellow pine forest zone extends from lakeshore at roughly 1,100 feet to about the 3,000 foot level.   The zone is readily distinguished by the presence of ponderosa pine.

The grand and Douglas fir (Canadian) zone extends from about 3,000 to 4,500 feet in altitude; western larch and lodgepole pine are the other two common trees found in this life zone.

The subalpine fir (Hudsonian) zone ranges from 4,500 to 6,500 feet in elevation.   Other common trees are the mountain hemlock, whitebark pine, Engelmann's spruce, and Lyall's larch.   In this zone are found the splendid alpine meadows.   At the upper limits of the zone, the trees become brushy shrubs (krummholz) as a result of the ongoing struggle to survive both the extremes of temperature and violent winds common at these elevations.

The alpine zone includes all the terrain above timberline. By definition, trees do not grow in this area. Specialized flowers survive and reproduce above the tree line, examples are the moss campion, Lyall lupine, and the golden fleabane. Shrubs such as luetkea also are found above the altitude where trees can survive (above 6,500 feet).

Animals (Zoology)

Life zones within the North Cascades National Park and associated areas are fairly sharply demarcated on the east side of the range. Birds, plants and animals tend to be found in particular life zones in many areas. However, in the North Cascades, there is considerable animal migration between the life zones. As snow melts, many animals migrate upward into the high country, returning to the valley floors when winter fills the high meadows with 20 to 30 feet of snow.

The animals most likely to be seen by hikers and shuttlebus riders in the Stehekin area are deer (Odocoileus). Mule deer (named for their large "mule-like" ears) predominate on the east side of the Cascade crest. Deer are found in season within all life zones since they migrate upward to the high meadows in the summer, returning to the lowland valleys in the winter. Males have antlers; the older the male deer, the larger and more branched are the rack of antlers. Female deer do not have horns.

The deer is a herbivore (browser) feeding on vegetation wherever available. Fawns are born in the spring, usually singly, but occasionally as twins. The fawn is almost odorless, thus protecting it from its enemies. The fawn is dappled during the first few months of life. Deer tend to be nocturnal, and are most easily seen early in the morning and late in the evening. All deer have pronouncedly plumed tails which they use as signalling devices.

Another common animal in the park is the American black bear (Euarctos). Large adults may weigh as much as 500 pounds. They are omnivorous and consume such extraordinary things as wasp's nests, skunk cabbage, huckleberries and blueberries, dead animals, young deer, salmon, and camper's food supplies. It should be stressed that these animals are at all times dangerous and unpredictable, particularly the female with cubs. Up to three cubs, each about the size of a rat, are born in late winter and remain with the mother for up to two years. Bears hibernate in winter and are rarely seen from December to February.

The true monarch of the peaks is the mountain goat (Oreamnos). These are the largest of the rock goats with deep but short and narrow bodies with heavy shoulders, long necks and large heads. They are pure white; the males have a long beard. These animals

Very young fawn

spend their entire lives in the high country, and are able to make their way with safety over rock faces and cliffs that would tax the ability of the bravest and most able human mountaineer. They rarely descend to the trees, but stay on the barest and bleakest mountain tops in all seasons and in all weather; however, occasionally a group will be seen in the lowland country, particularly near the shore of Lake Chelan, in the winter or early spring. They feed on mosses, lichens and whatever other stunted growth is available in the winter, and on the alpine meadow vegetation in the summer. The females retire in parties together to bear their young, and then stay away from the males for some weeks. During the rest of the year, they go about in small herds made up of all ages and sexes. It is generally an achievement to see one of these animals since they are almost never visible from roads or well-traveled areas.

The cougar, also known as the puma or mountain lion (Felis concolor), is the most widespread terrestrial mammal except for man. The cougar ranges from southeastern Alaska to Patagonia. Still unprotected in some states, and, indeed, still a bounty animal in Texas, the cougar is now protected in the Pacific Northwest where it is considered a game animal presently with season and kill limits. The mountain lion is secretive and elusive. Many persons who have spent years in the wilderness have never seen one (including the author who has tried unsuccessfully for 23 years to see a cougar in the wild). The cougar population of the state is presently estimated at 1,500 animals. Some years ago, five cougars were seen at one time on the Bridge Creek Bridge. Occasionally an animal must be encouraged to depart from under the house of a Stehekin resident.

Cougars lead largely solitary lives. The adult females and males live alone and fend for themselves. The female raises a litter of 2 or 3 kittens for about two years with no assistance from other adults. The kittens are able to kill small prey, such as rabbits, when only a few weeks old. Only one or two kittens usually survive to adulthood, and they may have trouble locating a suitable territory. The females are strongly territorial, defending their 5 to 15 square mile areas against other females. Males wander over larger areas, often overlapping the territories of two or three females. The displaced or young male searching for his own territory may have to fight for ground.

The scream of the cougar, likened to a woman's scream, generally indicates that the female is in heat. After mating, the pair remain together for about one week and then separate. The litter is born about three months later, usually in the late spring or early summer.

Cougar kill an average of about one deer every 7 to 10 days. They also kill smaller, more abundant prey, such as rabbits, more frequently. The killed animal is often cached, and later the cougar returns and feeds again. It has been learned that one of the critical advantages of cougar predation is that the animal selects the easiest prey (i.e., the infirm and diseased), therefore maintaining a healthier game herd.

The deer and the cougar are one of nature's ongoing systems of checks and balances. If the deer herds increase, the number of cougars increase; more cougar kill more deer; the deer herds decrease to within the limitations of the available forage; the cougars then also decrease. This feedback cycle prevents deer herds from becoming so numerous that they starve, and, as mentioned above, keeps the herds healthy by culling the diseased, injured, and aged animals.

Cougars very rarely attack man; campers in the Valley are more likely to be struck by lightning than to be assaulted by a mountain lion.

The two characteristic mammals of the high country are the pica, affectionately known as the conie, and the marmot. The pica (Ochonotonidae) are fluffy little egg-shaped animals with small rounded ears which are encountered among the loose rock of talus slopes. These animals are communal, and keep up a ceaseless high-pitched cheep or whistle, particularly when frightened. They collect masses of grass and other vegetable matter, making hay racks of it outside their holes in the rocks where they dwell. This is their food, and they spend much of their lives caring for it, carrying it below if rains are threatening, and bringing it out to dry again when bad weather passes. They feed on this food in the winter, when they live in their rocky homes buried under 20 or 30 feet of snow, but remain active nonetheless. They bear 4 or 5 young at a time.

The hoary marmot (Marmota) or whistler also inhabits talus slopes in the Hudsonian and Arctic-Alpine zones. They hibernate during the winter, awakening in late spring. They are vegetarians, feeding on the grasses and flowers of the high alpine meadows. They live in holes excavated under rocks, and in talus slopes. The marmot often will sit on a rock or outcropping near his hole or den and survey his domain; when disturbed, he emits a high-pitched shrill whistle which rises in pitch as whatever is disturbing to him comes closer. When danger threatens he disappears underground rapidly, only to reappear shortly thereafter, as these animals are very curious. Both marmots and conies are sometimes shot by unknowing individuals; both are protected animals even outside of the park boundaries, and a substantial fine can be levied on anyone killing them.

The porcupine (Erethizon) is often seen on trails and roads within the forested area of the park. Although slow moving and defenseless against an armed man, they exhibit a formidable defense to animal predators. An unwise aggressor will receive a paw or face full of spines that pierce his skin as they pull out of the porcupine. Although these spines are never "shot", once firmly implanted in the other animal, they are difficult to remove (as many dog owners know). In the wild, ultimate infection or penetration of a vital organ by a spine often is the ending for any animal sufficiently unwise to attack the porcupine. Porcupines are rodents with tremendous jaw power. They kill trees by "ringing" them for their sap content. They usually bear two young in the spring. These animals may be seen all year since they do not hibernate.

Other relatively common mammals found in the park and associated areas are the ground squirrel, racoon, beaver, and an occasional coyote. Weasels, rats, mice, moles, and shrews also inhabit the area.

One grizzly bear was probably identified in the park area in 1969. An occasional moose, elk, wolverine, marten, lynx and fisher may also be seen.

All animals within the park are protected and injuring or killing any animal within the park boundaries is a federal offense, punishable by fine or imprisonment. Hunting is allowed in the National Forest and National Recreational Areas subject to the laws of Washington.

Rattlesnakes are not uncommon in the Stehekin area. They are rarely found west of the river or lake, but are fairly common between Prince Creek and McGregor Mountain. Although they can swim readily and occasionally climb trees, the Stehekin rattlesnake is most commonly seen on the ground. There are approximately 30 species of rattlesnakes throughout the world, but the western rattlesnake (Crotalus viridis) is the only species of pit viper in the Stehekin area.

The rattle tends to frighten or warn creatures that might harm the snake. The sound is produced by vibrations of the tail, with the speed of vibration varying with the ambient temperature. The rattles are composed of horny material similar to that of fingernails; a new segment is produced with each skin shedding, not annually as was once believed. The approximate rate of rattle accumulation is three to four times a year in young snakes and twice a year in adults. The rattles are subject to loss by wear and tear, so very long strings are rare even in older snakes. Although most snakes rattle prior to striking, this cannot be guaranteed.

Rattlesnakes have a moderately keen sense of vision, particularly for moving objects. They also have an acute chemoreceptive sense of smell, and are alert to ground tremors, although they lack a sense of hearing. The rattlesnake is a pit viper; the facial pits are organs of acute sensitivity to minor differences in temperature. This is a valuable asset to the snake for preying on small but "warm blooded" mammals, particularly at night.

The body temperature of the rattlesnake is dependent on air and ground temperature. The rattlesnake seeks refuge when its body temperature is below 55 degrees F (13 C) or above 100 degrees F (38 C). Rattlesnakes are most active with a temperature range between 75 and 80 degrees F and tend to be nocturnal. Snakes mate in the spring and the young are born in the fall. There are usually between 3 and 12 young. The newborn rattler is encased in a membrane which it slits with a special tooth. The mother abandons the young within a few hours, leaving the small snake to fend for itself. The average rattlesnake lives 10 to 12 years. Natural enemies include coyotes, foxes, wildcats, hawks, and king snakes. Deer and goat sometimes kill rattlers by deliberately stamping on them with their hooves; however, by far the greatest killer of rattlesnakes is man, and his automobiles.

All rattlesnakes are venomous and therefore dangerous; however, almost all snakes will go out of their way to avoid a human if given an opportunity to do so. Use caution in snake country, particularly at night. Wear high boots and long pants. The treatment for an inflicted bite with evidence of poisoning consists of rest, use of a constricting band above the bite, incision and suction if the bite is located in a body area without blood vessels or tendons, and prompt hospitalization with early use of antivenin. (See *Mountaineering Medicine—A Wilderness Medical Guide* for more discussion of this somewhat controversial subject.)

Birds (Ornithology)

The birdlover will find that traveling in the North Cascades National Park is a rewarding experience. Current information indicates at least 225 species may be seen. Birds are found in all life zones, lowland valleys to alpine peaks. Because of altitude and climate, the crest of the Cascades forms a racial barrier. Many birds on the eastern slopes belong to the Rocky Mountain races; those on the west to the Pacific Coast races. Many birds wander after the breeding season, migrating vertically.

A number of birds of interest in the Stehekin Valley will be discussed at some length either because they are common or of unusual interest. These include the Harlequin Duck, White Tailed Ptarmigan, Rufous Hummingbird, Bald Eagle, Canada Goose, Gray Jay, Oregon Blue Grouse, and Western Tanninger. Other birds which may be often seen in the valley are the crow, Common Raven, woodpeckers, Mallard ducks, Great Blue Heron, Western Grebe, Common Loon, Common Goldeneye, Western Bluebird, Brown-headed Cowbird, American Goldfinch, and the House Finch. Park headquarters can provide a list of other birds in the area on request.

In the spring and early summer, there are usually Canada Geese nesting at the upper end of the lake; goslings can almost always be seen from May through July. Food for the Canada Goose consists of both vegetable and animal matter. Grain from stubble fields and grass with the roots form the staple of their diet. In the summer, they may eat small animals found in their favorite marshes, such as snails, tadpoles, and minnows. In the fall, one of the thrilling sights and sounds is to see a long V-shaped line of migrating geese, and hear the multiple honking noises that they make while flying.

Adults are roughly 40 inches long with their head and neck black, the body deep grey, the rump, tail, and quills black, and the ventral region white.

The American Golden Eagle is fairly common in the timberline regions of the Cascades, where there is suitable habitat, including usually an expanse of open country with an abundance of prey, and a rocky ledge or cliff on which to nest. Eggs are laid in the spring and the incubation lasts about 4 weeks. Eagles are subject to assaults by smaller, quicker birds.

To see an eagle soaring on high when it is on the hunt is to

Two ptarmigans

witness an example of the acuteness of its sense of sight to locate its prey. Suddenly with wings partly folded it plunges into a nose-dive, shooting earthward after its quarry, which may include marmots, rabbits, picas, chipmunks, squirrels, and other birds. The eagle will also eat carrion, such as dead or dying salmon. Its close relative, the Northern Bald Eagle, usually nests in a tall tree. In the fall and winter, the Bald Eagle is a scavenger feeding extensively on the dead salmon which accumulate along the rivers of Western Washington. Eagles are large birds, about 30-35 inches long with a wing spread of 6 to 7 feet.

The Oregon Blue Grouse, or Wood Grouse, is one of the best known game birds in the Stehekin area. It is found from sea level to timberline, with the birds generally in the lowland during the winter and in the high country during the summer. In the spring, the sound of a grouse thrumming is one of the lovely sounds of the mountains. With good fortune, it is possible to see the male making this courtship noise. Seeing grouse chicks is common. The female is fearless in protecting the chicks and will either actively attack a human who gets too close or will feign injury in an attempt to lead the person away from the chicks. Eggs are laid in the ground with little attempt at nest building. The grouse feeds on a variety of wild berries and other vegetation including salal, blueberries, and mountain ash. In addition, ants and grass-hoppers are also eaten. Alpine fir needles may also be a food source, particularly in the winter. Grouse are often approachable to within a few feet before flying. Occasionally, however, they burst upward with a loud, whirring noise, startling the hiker.

The White Tailed Ptarmigan is one of the most handsome and most approachable avian species in the Cascade Mountains. In the summer, it is a mottled brown color; in the winter, it is pure white. This alpine grouse remains in the high country all year and does not descend in the winter, except in the face of overwhelming storms. The birds are very approachable, and the author has many times walked within 2 to 6 feet of ptarmigan without great difficulty.

The ptarmigan is a classic example of protective coloration since its plumage harmonizes with the background in both summer and winter. The birds often react to danger by becoming motionless until the danger passes, which may be one of the reasons why they are easily approachable. The nest is usually located between 5,000 and 8,000 feet and is ordinarily found in the open surrounded by heather or other alpine plants. Eggs are laid late in the spring and, with luck, an observer can encounter two to ten chicks in the high country during the summer. By the middle of September, the chicks are almost fully grown. As with the Wood Grouse, the mother ptarmigan may attack humans if she feels the chicks are in danger. The food of this alpine bird is largely vegetable, including the leaves and flowers of the tiny alpine Buckwheat, leaves of Lyall's lupine, huckleberries, leaves and flowers of white and red "heather", and insects. Ptarmigan are scarce and should never be harmed. One of the real thrills of the alpine meadow is to encounter one of these "mountain grouse".

If you are fortunate, you may see the Harlequin Duck (Histrionicus histrionicus). This uncommon and shy duck spends summers on swift rivers of the west and may be seen with some frequency on the Stehekin River, particularly near the Harlequin Campground. The duck winters in the heavy surf along rocky ocean coasts. This aquatic bird is distinctively marked with a combination of red, blue, white, and black plumage. The female is smaller than the male. Nests are composed of feathers, dried leaves, moss, and lichens. The bird when inland feeds chiefly on aquatic insects. Along the coast, it eats crustaceans, mussels, and other marine animals. The Harlequin and its young are frequently encountered on high mountain streams on both sides of the Cascade Mountains.

The Rufous Hummingbird male has a brilliant, fiery red and orange throat. These birds migrate fantastic distances, appearing in the Valley in the spring and departing in the fall for Mexico and Central America. They are found from the lake to the highest peaks in the range. They are attracted by red colors and may approach a person wearing a red apparel item. They are an absolute flying marvel, being able to hover in one place like a helicopter, or dart here and there with seemingly miraculous speed and coordination. Nesting continues through May and a second brood may be raised later in the summer. Nests are covered with fresh, green moss. Courting hummingbirds may fight fierce and angry battles and, indeed, the bird may attack other larger birds. Hummingbird feeders, containing sugar and red pigment, are frequently utilized, particularly early in the spring before much vegetation is in flower. The standard diet, however, is nectar obtained from various flowering plants.

The Gray Jay, commonly known as the Camp Robber, is a handsome, large bird that inhabits the subalpine meadows in the summer. It will steal items of food from campsites which are left unguarded. The bird apparently eats pine nuts and insects when not subsisting off the handouts offered intentionally or otherwise by campers.

Perhaps the most unusual bird in the Stehekin area is the Water Ouzel or "Dipper". The Dipper is classically seen on an exposed rock in the middle of a turbulent stream; every few moments it dips or curtsies, a movement characteristic and unmistakable. It is seldom seen far from water. Occasionally the grey-blue bird disappears into the rushing water of the rapids; slightly smaller than a robin, it can move effectively under water and obtains its food from the bottom of rushing mountain streams. The nest of the Ouzel is usually located under a waterfall. The Dipper is undaunted by cold water, and may be seen in mountain streams even in winter. It is a real experience to sit beside a cascading torrent of water and watch a Water Ouzel negotiate the turbulent water in search of food.

The Western Tanninger is a strikingly colored bird with the head and neck bright orange or red, and the rest of the underparts bright yellow with the upper parts black. It is seen frequently in the spring. The birds eat primarily insects. Their favorite nest location is on the branch of a fir tree 15 to 50 feet above the ground.

Insects (Entomology)

After God created the North Cascades, He saw that they were perfect. Since perfection by divine decree can not be allowed in this world, it was then necessary to create the mosquito, the horse fly, and the yellow jacket!

Insects are one of the major drawbacks of the Stehekin area. With the exception of the yellow jacket, the universal rule in the

Stehekin Valley is that if an insect lands on you, slap it immediately. Yellow jackets unfortunately may sting even though killed; the best technique the author has discovered for dealing with yellow jackets is to take a deep breath and blow them off. Avoid leaving food attractive to yellow jackets near areas of human activity. The other common annoying insects are the No-See-Ums or biting gnats, horse flies, deer flies, and the ubiquitous mosquito.

Yellow jackets, hornets, and paper wasps are known for their potent sting and for their production of paper nests. The group is known as the social vespids. Nests are constructed underground where there is insulation from cold, on branches, tree limbs, or under the eaves of houses. The yellow jacket queen hibernates during the winter in a sheltered spot. In the spring she slowly comes to life, crawls forth into the sunshine and flies away, seeking a suitable place for a home. After drinking deeply, she begins construction of a small nest with a few cells. When the cells are finished, eggs are laid in each and when the eggs hatch, she hunts insects or other sources of food to feed the developing workers. Nectar, fruit juice, or other foods are all acceptable to the omnivorous yellow jacket.

Once the first generation of workers emerges, they take over all the work and the queen becomes simply an egg-layer. If the nest is underground, more earth is removed and the cavity is enlarged. Regardless of the nest location, more wood and fiber are collected and more tiers of brood cells are added. Paper walls always enclose and protect the entire structure. By autumn, the nest may be as large as a pumpkin and contains 2,000 or 3,000 short-tempered inhabitants. There is no defense for the unfortunate person who blunders into a yellow jacket's nest; the all important activity under those circumstances is immediate, rapid flight from the area.

Nests are practically impregnable during daylight hours, but can be dealt with, in almost total safety, by approaching after dark when all the inhabitants are inside and inactive. There is usually only one queen, although occasionally there is competition between queens for the nest; this contest ends in the death of one queen. In the fall, new queens and drones are produced and fly away and mate. The drones die and the queens seek places to hibernate. The parent colony gradually becomes less and less active, as the cold penetrates the earth and food is no longer available. Eventually, all the workers in the colony die, thus ending another annual chapter in the life of the yellow jacket.

There is no good remedy for the yellow jacket sting, which feels like the penetration of a red hot needle. Discomfort lasts from twelve hours to several days. Serious allergic reactions to stings do occur in susceptible individuals and can be life-threatening. Multiple stings can produce severe illness requiring hospitalization.   Removal of the stinger (if visible), cold applications, and over-the-counter pain medicine (such as aspirin) are the treatments of choice. Antihistamines may help somewhat.

There are no malaria-carrying mosquitoes in the Stehekin area. Serious disease from the bites of this insect are improbable here, although mosquito-borne virus infections of the brain affected over 2,000 people in the United States in 1975.

The common Culex mosquito lays its eggs in floating rafts anywhere there is stagnant water. Sites can include holes in trees, minor depressions in the forest floor, and rain barrels; boggy and swampy areas remaining after the high spring runoff are common breeding areas in the Valley.

The larvae or wrigglers are aquatic; they feed on algae and microscopic bits of organic debris. They project a respiratory tube through the water surface film to get air. The pupae, the next stage of development, also come to the surface for air. Both larvae and pupae are important food sources for fish and aquatic insects. The adult emerges from the pupae. Adults mate soon after emergence, after which the males die. Only the females suck blood; both sexes feed on plant juices.

The high mountain snow mosquitoes of the western United States are ice-age left-behinds. These mosquitoes lay their eggs once a year in pools formed from melting snow.   Originally adapted to the harsh cold climate of the Arctic, these insects were pushed south by advancing glaciers; they were forced to move up into the mountains following the post-glacial warming trend. At this time, isolated at high elevations, they are the principal mosquito species of the coniferous forests of western North America.

Most commerical insect repellants are generally effective for mosquitoes.

Biting midges are small to minute, mosquito-like insects that breed in aquatic and semi-aquatic environments.   The No-See-Ums, sand fleas, and gnats are included in this group. A blood meal is required for egg production; both males and females also obtain nectar from flowers. Most species lay their eggs in a gelatinous mass in the water or at water's edge; the larvae develop in these damp, wet places, feeding on decaying organic matter, dead insects, or newly hatched larvae of other insects. Being small, they are not easily seen and may be able to penetrate screens which are effective barriers for mosquitoes and larger biting insects.

Black flies also attack man. Immature stages are aquatic. Deer and horse flies are stout-bodied, powerful, and frequently large insects most commonly found around lakes, bogs, streams, and ponds. The eggs of most species are laid in masses on vegetation over or near the water. The larvae mature in damp or wet soil; in general, the larvae are also predaceous and cannibalistic. The adult females obtain nourishment both from blood meals and also from plant nectar, since sugar is necessary for their metabolism.

Commonly used insect repellants are ineffectual against the biting flies. Fortunately for the hiker, the flies are active during daylight only; in general, the hotter the weather, the more prevalent the flies.

Plants (Botany)

The hiker or climber who is so intent on reaching his destination in the mountains that he pays little attention to the many and varied flowering plants along his way is missing one of the greatest pleasures to be enjoyed in the North Cascades. The availability of color photography has assisted many people to become deeply interested in wildflowers. Observe them, but please do not pick them!

The trillium is a common early spring flower in the Valley. Most of the time, the blooms have withered when tourists arrive. However, trillium do bloom in the high areas later in the spring, and may be seen blooming near snowline in June. The flower can be recognized by its three white petals nestling between three broad green leaves; it grows to a height of about one foot. Overmature blossoms turn a brilliant violet. The leaves and flowers can not be separated; if the flower is picked, the plant will die and there will be no flower the following spring. It is most important therefore that the plants not be cut for inside display. Central seeds form in the late fall. The plant is shade tolerant, and is usually found under deep forest cover where humus and decaying wood have enriched the soil.

The forest is the habitat of some curious plants known as saprophytes, which are devoid of green chlorophyl and grow on decaying matter. Most conspicuous of these is the all white Indian pipe. The many flowered Indian pipe and pinesap are similar plants, which are red or tawny. Tallest of the saprophytes is the red and white barber pole or candy-stick. Pine drops is a white or pink plant with urn-shaped flowers. Three species of coral-root, members of the orchid family, also are saprophytic.

On open rocky slopes will be found sedums which have small fleshy leaves and yellow flowers. The rest of the plant sometimes is quite red. Here, too, will be found the penstemons with pink to purple tubular flowers.

Related to the above, but preferring wet places, are the red and yellow monkey-flowers. Along streams also will be found saxifrages bearing clusters of small white flowers. This, too, is the habitat of the alpine fireweed, prettier than its cousin of the burned-over areas.

We have left the big timber below and are in a place where the trees are in scattered clusters, the upper part of the Canadian zone. The spatulate leaves of the queen's cup bead lily cover the ground, the little six-petaled white flowers cradled among them. A tall shrub with clusters of white flowers is the Cascades azalea or white rhododendron. A showy clump of red flowers with yellow centers is the Sitka columbine. Blue lupines and bluebells give color harmony to the yellow of arnicas, wallflowers, groundsels and cinquefoils. Conspicuous by its size is the green false hellebore with broad, big-veined leaves. Another tall plant with spotted orange flowers is the beautiful Columbia lily. Bordering a shallow brook are clusters of creamy marsh marigolds, and shooting-stars with pink recurved petals.

The greatest display of flowers is found in the subalpine meadows near the limit of tree growth. Scarcely waiting for the snow to melt, the little glacier lilies carpet the meadows with yellow. The white sepals of the pasque flower appear, soon to be replaced by mop-like seed heads. Little white flowers of the narrow-leaved spring beauty are sprinkled about. By mid-July, the meadows are abloom with so many kinds of flowers that space is not available to name them all. Most common are the tall umbels of the white Sitka valerian and the dense white clusters of the bistort. Also present are pink daisy-like fleabanes, pedicularis, including the elephant head with curious little reddish up-turned trunks, scarlet paintbrush, mountain buttercups, and blue Jacob's ladders. The little spreading phlox covers rocky areas with its white to pink bloom. With companion flowers, these beautiful slopes are seen to rival man-made rock gardens.

Common evergreen shrubs of the high meadows are the red mountainheath, yellow mountainheath, and the white Merten's cassiope, all of which are generally called heathers.

Late season flowers are the many asters and the blue gentians. Due to extremes of weather at the upper limits of vegetation growth, the plants found here are dwarfed and are especially adapted to survive in a brief growing season. Climbers have been thrilled by the sight of a dense mass of tiny red flowers, the moss campion, frequently seen near the rocky summit of a mountain. Other plants which may be found at this elevation are Lyall's lupine, Tolmie saxifrage, silky phacelia, and golden fleabane.

The other prominent flowering plant of the Stehekin is the

balsamroot, which blooms on the rocky slopes of the Valley usually in May.   Blooming time may vary by several weeks, depending on snow level and temperature.   When in bloom, the floral display is brilliant with bright yellow flowers luxuriantly and exuberantly scattered over the relatively open forest floor.   The plant may bloom as late as July, high on the rocky bluffs.   By midsummer the leaves have dried and rustle in the wind, making a noise that, at times, may be mistaken for the rattle of a Western rattlesnake.

The most common tree in the Valley is the ponderosa pine.   Old large trees have thick reddish brown bark; younger smaller trees do not exhibit this esthetically enjoyable feature.   The tree has 5 to 8 inch long needles in bunches of three.   Cones are egg-shaped, 3 to 5 inches long, with a sharp spine on the back of each cone scale.   As might be expected, this tree is tolerant of heat and drought; in fact, it requires lots of sunshine for normal growth. The thick bark of old trees is quite resistant to fire.

The other common tree is the Douglas-fir, which is a misnomer since it is not a true fir as the complete seed cone falls to the ground when ripe.   Bark is corky and textured.   Needles are blueish-green; cones have forked bracts.   This tree requires more moisture than the ponderosa pine.

The cones of the true firs (silver, grand, noble, and subalpine) disintegrate at maturity leaving spike-like cores standing upright on the higher branches.

Three other species of pine inhabit the east slopes of the Cascades.   The lodgepole pine has short needles in clusters of two and very small cones.   The white pine is a tall symmetrical tree bearing very long slim cones and with five needles in each cluster. A tree of the high ridges and passes is the whitebark pine.   Usually rough in appearance, it has light gray bark, thick short cones, and needles in clusters of five.

The western hemlock is found below 4,500 feet and can easily be identified by the top, which tends to droop to one side.   Needles and cones are very short.   At higher elevations, the mountain hemlock is found.   It has brown, deeply furrowed bark.   The slender cones are 1.5 to 3 inches long.

Two cedars are resident in the Cascades: the western red cedar which is found to about 4,500 feet, and the Alaska or yellow cedar which inhabits the subalpine areas.   Both have stringy bark, that of the yellow cedar being light gray.   Both cedars have scaly, overlapping leaves.

A tree with scaly bark, stiff needles and ragged cones is the Engelmann spruce.   Western yew has a rough appearance, rather smooth reddish bark, short needles, and red berries in the fall.

Hikers in the upper valleys in the fall will be impressed by the brilliant fall color of the vine maple and Douglas maple. Vine maple has 7 to 9 sharp pointed lobed leaves that are 3 to 4 inches across. The leaves may begin to turn red or yellow as early as mid-summer. They produce an unforgetable display of color in October. When it grows in clearings, or in avalanche chutes, vine maple can form a bushy, multi-stemmed tree that is 20 to 30 feet tall. The vine maple is tolerant of shade and grows as forest undercover, whereas the Douglas maple needs open sunlight. The Douglas maple leaf is a bit smaller with only 3 to 5 main points. Both maples are a favorite food of deer.

The leaves of the quaking aspen, bright green above and silvery beneath, tremble and whisper when stirred by the slightest breeze. Small groves of aspen are found tucked away in the high valleys of the Stehekin drainage. Their leaves turn yellow, golden, and occasionally even reddish in the fall, making the mountain landscape more splendid. Aspen can be identified both by its sound and by the presence of leaf motion in even a minimal wind. The bark is smooth and a cream-colored white.

A common and spectacular tree in the lower Valley is the Pacific dogwood. There are a large number of these trees in the Stehekin area; one scenic specimen is found at the base of Rainbow Falls. There is also a large grove of trees at the Rainbow Creek Bridge two miles from the Valley floor. This is the most beautiful flowering tree in the Valley, although its true "flowers" are small, greenish, and inconspicuous. These plain flowers, however, are set in a cluster of creamy, white floral leaves creating the effect of a cream-colored blossom 4 to 6 inches across. By fall, the inconspicuous true flowers have ripened into a cluster of bright red fruits about one inch across, nestled among leaves that have turned red and purple. Occasionally a dogwood will even flower again if there is an extended Indian summer.

This tree is unusual because it is able to survive and bloom in the forest understudy. It is very shade tolerant and needs little sunlight. The tree is a hardwood and apparently the wood was considered especially suited for skewers or "dags" and, in time, dagwood became dogwood. In the Valley, the trees bloom maximally about Memorial Day.

Those hikers who reach the alpine meadows at the heads of the various secondary valleys radiating from the Stehekin will see a number of interesting trees. Each tree has a rather definite nitch and appearance in the alpine meadows. However, near the upper range of timberline, the trees become dwarfed, stunted and atypical; this phenomena is called krummholz. High alpine trees include subalpine fir, Engelmann spruce, whitebark pine, and alpine larch.

The subalpine fir is easily identified by its cathedral spiral-like shape. This growth form has obvious advantage to enable the tree to resist heavy coatings of ice and snow in the deep winter.

Clearly the most unusual tree in the area is alpine or Lyall's larch. This tree grows in small open stands, rarely below 5,500 feet. The needles are a soft, pale, luxuriant green in the summer. This tree is one of the very few deciduous conifers (i.e., a cone-bearing tree that loses its needles in winter). One of the crowning magnificent sights in the North Cascades occurs in the last week of September and first week in October, when the larch turns a golden yellow before it drops its needles. When backlit by the sun, the trees glow. Larch is found in a north-south distance of only about 120 miles in the Cascades. The tree is never found below 5,000 feet and cannot be grown in cultivation in lowland areas, presumably because it is intolerant of heat. It is of interest that of the world's ten larch species, nine grow at timberline either in the high mountains or in the Arctic tundra; the exception is the western larch.

Larch trees may reach 3 feet in diameter, 70 to 80 feet in height, with an age of 500 to 700 years. The largest known alpine larch is in a steep rocky basin at 6,200 feet elevation above Lake Chelan; it is 6.3 feet thick and 94 feet tall. Alpine larch is the first tree to colonize glacial morrains and high barren alpine areas from which the ice and snow have recently receded. Because of the harsh conditions, growth rates are slow. A small Alpine larch may be only two inches high, but 10 years old. Anyone who has walked in a golden larch forest in the fall will never forget the experience.

Lake Chelan

The name *Chelan* is derived from a Wapato Indian word meaning "deep water". This body of water is the largest natural lake in Washington. It is the second deepest lake in the United States. During summer, the lake level is 1,100 feet above sea level. The original elevation of the lake was 1,079 feet; the lake level was raised 21 feet in 1928 by a dam still in place slightly downstream from the town of Chelan.

The water level drops as low as 1,085 feet at times. When the lake is this low, substantial mud and sand flats are exposed at the upper end of the lake. When full, the lake has an area of almost 52 square miles, and is 50.4 miles (82 km) long with an average width of about one mile. There are numerous tributaries entering the lake, with the major drainages being Railroad Creek on the west, Prince Creek on the east, and the Stehekin River at the head of the lake.

The principal fish species in the lake are rainbow, cut-throat, silver, and eastern brook trout, and Dolly Varden.

Sonar studies of the lake made by J. T. Whetten of the

Lake Chelan from the hills above Stehekin

University of Washington Oceanography Department have indicated that there are two basins separated by a shallow constriction. The Lucerne Basin at the upstream end of the lake is substantially deeper and sediment on the lake bottom is relatively thin except at the Stehekin River delta at the upper end. The Wapato Basin at the southern end of the lake is shallow, but contains thick sediments on the bottom. The narrows which separates the two basins is underlaid by bedrock and land slide deposits.

The difference in water depth between the basins and the difference in sediment in the basins is theoretically due to the actions of two different glaciers; see the section on geology. Whetten's studies indicated the deepest portion of the lake was midway between Big Goat and Nobby Creeks, where the depth is 1528 feet (466 meters); this depth is 426 feet (133 meters) below sea level. There is some disagreement about the maximum depth of the lake; the book "Lakes of Washington" (Eastern volume) states that the deepest place in the lake is near its center off the mouth of Falls Creek, and cites a depth of 1,605 feet.

Stehekin Landing

Stehekin Landing

The structures in Sehekin in 1980 from southeast to northwest (i.e., from right to left as visualized by a person coming into Stehekin on the Lady of the Lake) are as follows:

1) Ranger's living quarters
2) the former Golden West Lodge, currently a Park Service information and visitor center (here overnight camping permits are issued; it is also the location for evening illustrated lectures)
3) small arts and crafts gift shop
4) photographic supply store
5) grocery store
6) snack bar
7) south portion of the North Cascades Lodge
8) restaurant and restrooms
9) main or north portion of the North Cascades Lodge
10) Post Office (in the bottom story); in the upper story is another Park Service interpretative center and the Ranger Station.
11) public laundry and shower; entry is on the southeast side of "A" frame; there is a sign on the building.

North of this structure, there are several private houses and the Purple Campground.

Stehekin Road

Beyond the campground, the twenty-three mile road continues northwest and ends at Cottonwood Camp. This road has been aptly described as beginning at the lakeshore and dead-ending in paradise. Presently the road may be hiked, bicycled, power-cycled, or, for the average visitor, traversed in one of the Park Service operated shuttlebuses. Permanent residents are allowed to have their own cars, so there is some private traffic on the road also, as well as vehicles of the Park Service work and ranger crews.

Presently, there are four shuttlebus departures a day from the restaurant to High Bridge ten miles away. A large, somewhat dilapidated bus is utilized for this part of the journey. Three daily trips go from High Bridge to Cottonwood Camp (road end).* Those going beyond High Bridge on the road change into small vans at that point for the journey to Cottonwood Camp. It takes about one hour to reach High Bridge and an additional hour to reach Cottonwood Camp. Shuttlebus schedules are prominently posted at the restaurant, ranger stations, and at trailheads; frequency of service varies early and late in the season, and often from year to year.

From Purple Camp, the road follows the lakeshore for about 1 mile and then enters wooded, somewhat swampy country at the northwest end of the lake. At 1.8 miles, the side road to Silver Beach cuts off to the left. At 2 miles, the side road to the Stehekin River Resort forks off the main road, again to the left. At approximately the 3 mile mark, the one-room Stehekin School, a registered historical landmark, is passed on the right. The Stehekin Community Building is just across the road from the school. A few feet further is Rainbow Creek, and shortly thereafter, the .1 mile spur road to Rainbow Falls goes to the right. The short walk from the loop roadhead to the base of the falls can be easily hiked by anyone. Standing in the spray of the falls, particularly in the spring when the snow melt is substantial and the dogwoods are blooming, is an experience long to be remembered.

A little beyond the 4 mile mark at the end of the blacktop, the road divides with the left fork crossing the Stehekin River to reach Harlequin Camp and the north trailhead of the Stehekin River Trail, the Stehekin Airport, Company Creek trailhead, and ultimately to a number of private residences on the southwest side of the river.

The main road continues upriver. There is a large talus and boulder slope at the site of the road junction. At 8 miles, the road passes the Courtney Homestead. The original Ray Courtney residence is on the left, and the newer Courtney house is across the pasture on the right. At 9.5 miles, the Bullion Loop Trail, and Old Wagon Trail to Coon Lake trailheads are passed. At 10.4 miles is the High Bridge Guard Station; the National Park boundary is at High Bridge itself. Just before the Guard Station, Agnes Creek joins the Stehekin on the left. The Agnes Gorge, Agnes Creek, Coon Lake, and McGregor Mountain Trails start very close to, or at, the High Bridge Guard Station. Primitive restrooms exist at this point.

Further upriver, the road deteriorates, but the scenery improves. Fishing is good in the Stehekin River and its tributaries after the spring runoff diminishes. Campsites are located at High

*No shuttlebus is scheduled above High Bridge in 1981 due to road washout. Check with ranger for availability.

Bridge, Dolly Varden, Bridge Creek, Shady Creek, and there are two separate camp areas at Cottonwood. Between High Bridge and Cottonwood are the upper end of the Old Wagon Road, and the Bridge Creek, Goode Ridge, Park Creek, and Flat Creek trailheads. The trail to Cascade Pass and Horseshoe Basin starts at the road end. Road distances from High Bridge are: Tumwater Bridge, 1.1 miles; Coon Lake Wagon trailhead, 1.5 miles; Bridge Creek, 4.6 miles; Park Creek, 7.1 miles; Cottonwood, 12 miles. It is usually late in the spring before the upper portion of the road is passable. It is wise to inquire at the Park Service office if planning a hike over Cascade Pass or down Bridge Creek prior to making final trip preparations.

The Stehekin River begins a few inches east of the crest at Cascade Pass. By the time it cascades downward from Pelton Basin in a series of waterfalls, it is a vigorous creek. Named major tributaries are Flat, Park, Bridge, Agnes, Company, Rainbow, and Boulder Creeks. It does not flow far as rivers go, perhaps 25 miles until it empties into Lake Chelan. The lake feeds into the Columbia River; eventually the water reaches the ocean between Astoria, Oregon and Fort Canby, Washington. Water dropping a few inches to the west of the Cascade Pass crest enters Puget Sound via the Skagit River.

The North Cascades are a young range as mountains go, born as a result of the oceanic crust underthrusting continental margins. The sharpness and height of the alpine topography speaks to the youth of the cordillera, as does nearby vulcanism, and frequent earthquakes. Recent glaciation has sculpted the North Cascades, accounting for the horns of the peaks, the steep headwalls below the passes, the cirque lakes, and the U-shaped valleys. The mountains around the Valley have been aptly termed "The Wilderness Alps of the Stehekin".

One peak commonly seen by the visitor is Castle Peak, across from Stehekin. Rising to 7,900 feet, seemingly straight up from the lakeshore, the peak often is reflected in the lake early in the day when the wind is still.

McGregor Mountain at 8,100 feet dominates the up-river view of the Stehekin Valley. Peaks in the Cascade Pass area include Boston, Sahale, Buckner, Magic, and Booker, ranging in altitude from 8,400 to 9,200 feet.

The highest peak in the park area is Goode Mountain (9,300 feet), located between Park Creek and the north fork of Bridge Creek. The highest non-volcanic peak in the North Cascades is Bonanza (9,511 feet), between Company and Railroad Creeks in the Glacier Peak Wilderness Area. The highest nearby peak is Glacier Peak (10,541 feet). Mt. Baker (10,778 feet) is the highest peak in the North Cascades.

Helpful Hints for Visitors

Winter weather is generally cold with the first snow usually falling in Stehekin about December 1 and melting off sometime in March. Spring comes relatively early; daytime temperatures are pleasant in the Valley by late April or early May. Summer weather in Stehekin can be oppressively hot, with temperatures in the high 90's relatively common in late July and early August. Fall is perhaps the most delightful season, with pleasant daytime temperatures, superb hiking conditions, and fall color.

The mountains east of Stehekin are generally snow-free to a degree making hiking possible by mid- to late-June; the mountains west of Stehekin do not become snow-free until about July 15 in an average year. This is because snowfall is substantially greater to the west of the Cascade Crest than it is east of the crest.

The generally best weather in the high mountain areas is from July 15 to August 15. Rain can occur at any time, particularly at or west of the crest, and storms may continue for several days, even in mid-summer. East of the crest particularly, late afternoon thunderstorms are not uncommon in mid-summer. All overnight campers should be prepared to cope with rain. High in the mountains, snow can occur any day of the year and significant snowfall begins about October 1, but unseasonable snow storms may occur in September.

Forty-one campgrounds have been identified in the Stehekin District of the Park and Recreation Area. A list of these campgrounds, available from the Park Service office, gives the elevation, location (section, range, and township), and a very brief description of each. Additional data about campsites is often contained in the trail notes for a particular trail described in this book.

There are a number of day hikes which can be made from Stehekin or various points along the Stehekin Road. A small rucksack or day pack should be carried. In the rucksack should be a first aid kit, water bottle, food, insect repellant, and extra clothes. Temperatures can change dramatically in the high country within a few hours; one can start in a T-shirt in the heat and five hours later be in drenching rain, or even snow. It is important to be prepared for these dramatic changes in temperature and precipitation. Hypothermia (exposure) can kill rapidly. (See "Mountaineering Medicine - A Wilderness Medical Guide" for other information about hypothermia.) Other useful items or emergency gear which should be in your pack include a map and compass, waterproof matches and a firestarter, sunglasses, pocket knife, flashlight, and a whistle.

Winter scene at Stehekin

Overnight backpackers obviously need more extensive equipment. A light waterproof alpine tent is an essential in the North Cascades in view of the unpredictable weather. Down sleeping bags are recommended, but must be enclosed in a waterproof container in order to keep them dry. Fiberfill sleeping bags are heavier and not as warm as down, but work better than down when wet. A waterproof pack cover that is durable and effective is recommended also. Fires are inappropriate or prohibited in many areas; a lightweight camp stove is an essential. Raingear and extra clothing for warmth are also mandatory. Good boots, well broken in before arrival, are another important item. Trails on the east side are drier than on the west, but mud or snow can be encountered any place in the mountains. Nights are cool in the high country, even in mid-summer. Remember, when you start in the valley, all trails go up, at a time when the pack is heaviest; a conditioning program prior to arrival is mandatory for exploration of the high country.

Fishing at the head of Lake Chelan generally requires a boat, although one can fish from the docks around Stehekin, or from the lakeshore. Most high lakes contain fish; supplementing a spartan backpacker diet with fried trout is delightful! A Washington license is required; licenses can be obtained in Stehekin or at sporting goods stores before arrival.

Fishing is very poor in the lower five miles of Agnes Creek because of the substantial amounts of glacial flour (fine powder produced by glacier grinding base rock) in the river. Boulder Creek may disappear into the ground before reaching the main river after the high spring runoff. If one hikes upstream, there is good fishing for the first 3 to 4 miles.

Fishing is good in the entire Bridge Creek drainage. Since the gorge above the road bridge is dangerous, it is best to hike upstream along the Bridge Creek Trail to reach fishing areas. Fishing is reasonably good in Company Creek, although the fish tend to be small. Devore Creek contains lots of fish. Flat Creek has fairly large cutthroats, but because of the log jams and dense undergrowth, one has to work for results. Park Creek contains fish throughout, but is brushy in its upper reaches. The lower portion has falls and a steep gorge which makes it impassable. There is reasonable fishing above the falls in Rainbow Creek. Fishing in the main Stehekin is good up to the falls coming down from Pelton Lake. In season, spawning trout from Lake Chelan ascend the river. Red colored silver trout can be seen in side pools along the river in the fall. The best fishing is in the late summer and early fall when water levels are lower. Flies are effective lures.

The Park Service office has a list of lakes in the Stehekin District, and includes elevation, location, and brief comments. Also available is a list of mountains with elevation, location, and very brief comments about each.

All overnight campers should protect food supplies against bears and other animals. Many of the campsites which have had bear problems are equipped with a bear cable, sometimes with stringers. All campers should carry about 40 feet of nylon cord. Before retiring for the night, all food supplies should be placed in the pack or other suitable container and strung over the bear cable. If there is no cable, hang your food on a tree limb at least 10 feet above the ground and 5 feet from the trunk of the tree. Supplies left in camp, if no one is present, should be processed in a similar manner.

The black bear is far less dangerous than the grizzly. Although many campers have lost food to bears, injury from bear attacks has been negligible; however, it is wise to not attract bears by keeping all food out of reach. In addition, never get between a mother bear and her cubs. A bear attack is not uncommon under these circumstances.

Limited transportation has preserved the Valley from engulfment by the outside world. The frustrations of travel are more tolerable under those circumstances. There is no scheduled air service. Chelan Airways offers charter service in float planes capable of carrying 3 and 5 people, with a minimum of 2 and 4 persons per flight. The current tariff is $25 per person one way. Flight time is about 30 minutes. The boat takes over 4 hours from

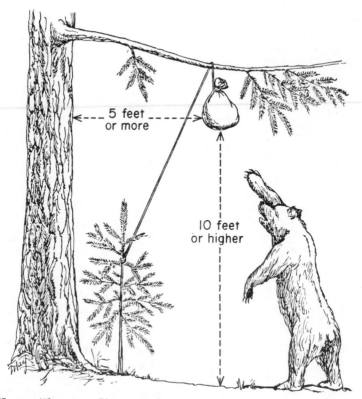

5 feet
or more

10 feet
or higher

How to "bearproof" a campsite

Chelan and almost 3 hours from 25 Mile Creek to make the trip to Stehekin. Current roundtrip fare from Chelan is $12.50; from 25 Mile Creek is $11.50. Anticipate inflationary increases as time passes. The boat runs Monday, Wednesday and Friday all year; there is no Sunday service from about January 1 to February 15. Daily boat service begins about May 15 and terminates about October 15.

Experienced pilots with appropriate aircraft can use the rather primitive airstrip about 4 miles from Stehekin. There are several public docks in the area for private boats. Perhaps most pleasant in season is to walk in; there are at least half a dozen ways to do so, some of which require use of the shuttlebus system. Shuttle rates are $1 per day currently. (See Trails Section.)

Winter services available at Stehekin are limited. Housekeeping cabins are available; you may need to bring all your food for your winter visit.

During the summer, there are slide programs conducted by the park rangers most evenings at the Golden West Lodge.

Most drivers of vehicles will give you a ride if you wish one while walking the road. Some walkers do not wish rides. If you do want a ride, face the oncoming car and stop walking to indicate that you wish a lift.

Please respect the rights of private landholders. Although most of the Valley is in the public domain, some land remains in private ownership. Be courteous and considerate toward the Stehekin community.

Hunting is allowed in the Lake Chelan National Recreation Area, but not in the North Cascades National Park. Recreationists should use caution in the Recreation Area during the fall hunting season. Avoid brushy areas, use high visibility clothing, and make noise (sing, whistle, or carry a tinkling bell). Dates of the fall hunting season are set each year by the state.

Challenging mountain climbing is easily available. Those contemplating climbs should refer to a standard reference source, such as guides written by Fred Beckey. Most climbs in the Cascades involve ascents on snow or ice and scrambles on rotten rock. The use of an ice ax is essential, and the ability to do a self-arrest is mandatory. All rock hand and foot holds should be carefully tested before placing weight on them; there is practically no solid rock anywhere in the North Cascades. Climbing parties should register with the park ranger on duty at the Golden West Lodge before ascents. High camps on ice, snow, and bare rock for practical purposes have no environmental impact. Those planning climbs in the Cascade Pass area should discuss potential high campsites with a ranger prior to departure, since the Cascade Pass area is closed to camping.

There are many opportunities for photography. One good rule in the North Cascades is if you can see it, photograph it immediately because you may not be able to see it later. Scenes with snow and ice require one f-stop down compared to standard exposure (i.e., f-16 rather than f-11). Deep forest shots are very difficult on sunny days, particularly with color film, in view of the marked light contrasts. In the woods, photography is best done on hazy or foggy days when the light is more uniform.

Stehekin is a special place! The uniqueness of the Valley and its surroundings can only be maintained by dedicated efforts by all concerned, including visitors, Park Service people, and residents. Nowhere else is there another place like this; hopefully the splendor that is here will be available to our progeny. Let no one say, and say it to your shame, that all was beauty here until you came!

Trails of the Stehekin Valley

Climb the mountains and get their good tidings.
—John Muir

Trails Foreword

The footpaths which can be reached from Stehekin without crossing a road are summarized in the material to follow. If walked by the author, the date that the trail was evaluated is included. If no date is indicated, other sources also were used to prepare the description. Permits are required in the Lake Chelan National Recreation Area, North Cascades National Park, and Glacier Peak Wilderness Area if overnight stays are planned. The permits can be obtained at Stehekin, Chelan, Marblemount, or at forest service ranger stations on the west side of the Glacier Peak Wilderness Area.

Trails change over the years, occasionally due to natural events, but more commonly due to human activities. It is always wise to check with the responsible land management authority beforehand to determine if significant changes have occured since this guide book was written. The author would appreciate any major inaccuracies being called to his attention.

Camping is allowed currently only in formal campsites in the National Park and in the Lake Chelan NRA. Exceptions are made for wilderness explorers who camp at least .5 mile from any trail and 1 mile from any designated campsite. Wilderness rangers patrol most areas to assist campers and to assure compliance with regulations.

It goes without saying that wilderness etiquette will be followed. Treat the land gently at all times. *Take only photos; leave only tracks.*

Trails generally are listed in geographical order, starting southwest of Stehekin and continuing in clockwise direction. (See overall map of trails on pages 50—51.) The difficulty rating of the trail is based on distance and elevation gain, usually within the following categories:

Rating	Round trip	Elevation gain	Time
EASY (E)	less than 1 mile	minimal	few minutes
MODERATELY EASY (ME)	2—5 miles	100'—300'	1—2 hours
MODERATE (M)	3—7 miles	500'—1500'	2½ hrs.—1 day
MODERATELY STRENUOUS	7—12 miles	2000'—5000	full day
STRENUOUS (S)	10—30 miles	2200'—6000'	½ day— 2—3 days

Easy—Anyone who can walk at all can do the trail;
Moderately Easy—The elderly, infirm, or ill may have difficulty;

Looking south from Stehekin

Moderate—Elderly, infirm, or ill should not attempt; can be walked by anyone in reasonable health;

Moderately Strenuous—A physical conditioning program is advised prior to attempting the full walk; walkers should be healthy;

Strenuous—Conditioning is essential; hikers should be in good health and experienced.

Ratings are for the entire trail. For example, the Lakeshore Trail is classed as moderate for its 17.2 miles, but a short section from the boat landing down lake could be classed as easy or moderately easy depending on the distance hiked and the walking speed. Hiking times are for round trips, unless otherwise indicated. Times are based on an average rate of two miles per hour (1½ miles an hour going up; 3 miles an hour on the level or descending, unless the tread is bad enough to slow the normal pace). Rest stops, recreational activities (e.g., photography), poor trail conditions, or different hiking rates would change the times.

Trails distances are given in miles; the following conversion table may be helpful for those who think better in the metric system:

> 328 feet = 100 meters
> .1 mile = 528 feet = 161 meters
> .631 miles = 3281 feet = 1000 meters (one kilometer)
> 1.0 mile = 5280 feet = 1.61 km (kilometer)

Trails to the east of the valley over 5,000 feet usually have snow until late June; footpaths closer to the crest of the Cascades may have snow in places in August. Hikers should have boots with Vibram lug soles and the experience to safely kick steps in snow slopes. Carrying an ice ax is strongly recommended, and hikers must know how to use it for self-arrest and perhaps for chopping steps in ice. The self-arrest technique to stop a slide on snow should be learned under supervision beforehand.

Trails of the Stehekin River Valley

Italic indicates brief descriptions of adjacent trails

Alphabetical List of Trails

(Continued on next page)

Access Trails to Stehekin Valley

FROM THE NORTH
Bridge Creek (PCT)—From North Cascades Highway
Thunder Creek (via Park Creek Pass)

FROM THE WEST
Cascade Pass

FROM THE SOUTHWEST
PCT— Suiattle Pass (via Agnes Creek/PCT)
Spider Meadow—Suiattle Pass (via Agnes Creek/PCT)
Suiattle Trail—Miner's Ridge (via Agnes Creek/PCT)

FROM THE SOUTHEAST
Lucerne—Holden—Railroad Creek—Suiattle Pass (Agnes Creek,
or cross-country via Company Creek)

FROM THE EAST
Copper Pass (via Bridge Creek/PCT)
Eagle Creek (via Summit Trail)
East Fork Buttermilk (via Summit Trail)
Reynolds Creek (via Boulder Creek)
South Creek (via McAlester Pass)
Summer Blossom (via Summit Trail)
Twisp Pass (via Bridge Creek/PCT)
War Creek (via Summit Trail)
West Fork Buttermilk (via Summit Trail)

Trails, According to Difficulty

	Distance (miles)		Elevation	Time. *(see listed distance)*
	*RT**	*One-way*	gain (feet)	
EASY				
Rainbow Falls	¼ mile			10 min.
MODERATELY EASY				
Agnes Gorge	5		300	2 hrs.
Bullion Loop	1.7		200	¾ hr.
Rainy Lake	2		100	¾ hr.
MODERATE				
Coon Lake/Wagon Rd.	3.2		700	1½ hrs.
Flat Creek	6.6		500	3 hrs.
Horseshoe Basin	3		1150	4 hrs.
Lakeshore Trail		17	3000	2 days
N. Fk. Bridge Ck.	14		1400	1 day
Rainbow Loop	5		750	2¼ hrs.
Stehekin River	8		200	3 hrs.
MODERATELY STRENUOUS				
Agnes Creek	35		4400	3-4 days
Bridge Creek		12.2	2300	6 hrs.
Cascade Pass	10		2650	5 hrs.
Copper Pass	8.4		2400	4½ hrs.
Park Creek Pass	16		3800	8 hrs.
Prince Ck.: N. Fk.; Mid. Fk.		9;11	4500; 5500	1½ days
Rainbow Lake		11	5000+	1 day
Stiletto Meadows	7		2300+	5½ hrs.
Summit Trail		30	8500	3-4 days
Twisp Pass	8.6		2200	4 hrs.
STRENUOUS				
Boulder Creek	22		5600	2 days
Company Creek	29		5500	2 days
Devore Creek	20		5400	2 days
Fish Creek: N.Fk.; E. Fk.		6.6;9.7	4300; 5300	1 day
Goode Ridge	11		4600	1 day
McAlester Pass	20,17†		2200	2 days
McGregor Mtn. (summit)	16		6500	2 days
Purple Pass		7.8	5800	1 day
Trapper Lake	1.5		1400	5 hrs.

*=Roundtrip † *Distances from Stehekin Road and North Cascades Highway, respectively.*

Location Map for

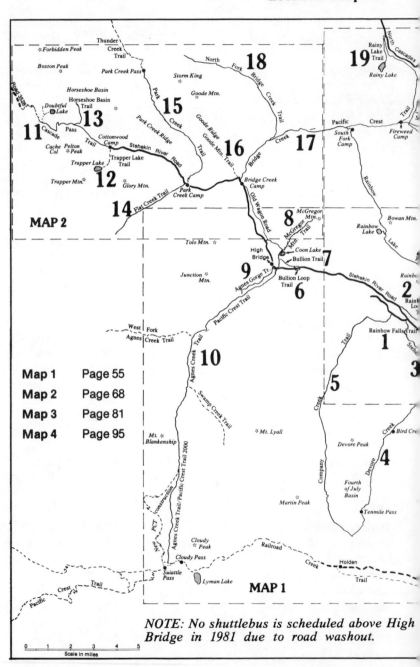

Forbidden Peak

Boston Peak

Thunder
Creek
Trail

Park Creek Pass

North

18

19

Rainy
Lake
Trail

Rainy Lake

Storm King

Goode Mtn.

Horseshoe Basin

Horseshoe Basin
Trail

Doubtful
Lake

15

Pacific   Crest

South
Fork
Camp

Fireweed
Camp

11

Cascade
Pass

13

Cache
Col

Pelton
Peak

Cottonwood
Camp

Stehekin   River   Road

Trapper Lake
Trail

16

Bridge

Creek

17

Rainbow

Bowan Mtn.

Rainbow
Lake

Lake

Trapper Lake

Trapper Mtn.

12

Glory Mtn.

Park
Creek Camp

Bridge Creek
Camp

14

Flat Creek Trail

Tolo Mtn.

High
Bridge

8

McGregor
Mtn.

McGregor
Mtn. Trail

Coon Lake

Bullion Trail

7

MAP 2

Junction
Mtn.

9

Agnes Gorge Tr.

Bullion Loop
Trail

6

Stehekin   River   Road

Rainbo

Rain

2

West   Fork

Agnes   Creek Trail

Pacific Crest Trail

Rainbow Falls Trail

1

3

Map 1   Page 55

Map 2   Page 68

Map 3   Page 81

Map 4   Page 95

Agnes Creek Trail

10

Swamp Creek Trail

5

Company

Devore

Creek

Bird Cre

Mt.
Blankenship

Mt. Lyall

Devore Peak

Fourth
of July
Basin

4

Martin Peak

Tenmile Pass

Agnes Creek Trail/Pacific Crest Trail 2000

PCT   construction   New

Cloudy
Peak

Railroad

Holden

Cloudy Pass

Suiattle
Pass

Lyman Lake

MAP 1

Pacific   Crest   Trail

Creek

Trail

*NOTE: No shuttlebus is scheduled above High
Bridge in 1981 due to road washout.*

0 1 2 3 4 5
Scale in miles

Stehekin Valley Trails

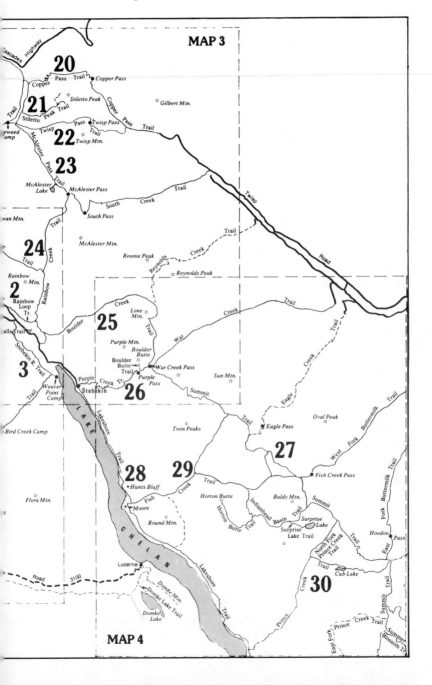

Trail Information

Rainbow Falls

1

Round trip: 200 yards
Elevation gain: Minimal
High point: 1400'
Hiking time: 10 minutes
Difficulty: Easy
USGS *Stehekin*
Green Trails *Stehekin*

Maps 1, 3

This trail runs from the Rainbow Falls spur road to the base of the falls. It is 100 yards long, and easy. It permits a close-up view of 312' Rainbow Falls.

In the spring, there is a blooming dogwood near the end of the trail. During the spring runoff, the amount of mist in the area is substantial, making photography difficult. Later in the year, when the stream volume decreases, photographic possibilities improve. In low water, it is possible to bathe safely in the pools below the falls. There are picnic tables near the falls and it is a delightful place to eat lunch.

The Rainbow Mist Trail above the falls has been closed for several years due to hazards associated with the heavy spray in the area. This short loop trail went up steeply, permitted different views of the falls, and showed the changes in plant life in the areas where the mist reached as compared to the dry areas where the spray from the falls did not penetrate.   (August 1979)

Rainbow Loop Trail

2

Round trip: 5 miles
Elevation gain: 750'
High point: 2150'
Hiking time: 2¼ hours
Difficulty: Moderate
USGS *Stehekin*
Green Trails *Stehekin*

Maps 1, 3

Rainbow Falls

The south trailhead begins .3 mile beyond the bridge crossing Rainbow Creek (2.7 miles from the road). The trailhead is signed. From this point, the trail runs 2.5 miles to rejoin the Stehekin Road .2 mile beyond the Company Creek Bridge; this trailhead is signed also.

With the exception of one or two areas where it is possible to step out onto a bluff via a scrabble trail, there are few views on the 2.5 mile northwest portion of the loop. There are no camping places. In the spring at least, water is available at several places. The altitude gain is 750′. The up-time is 1¼ hours and the down-time is 1 hour, for a total loop time of 2¼ hours.

The main value of the north loop is that one does not need to retrace steps if walking to the bridge over Rainbow Creek. However, the south route up via the Rainbow Trail is far more scenic and is mandatory for a one-way route, and may be desirable to use in both directions. (May 1978)

Stehekin River Trail

3

Round trip: 8 miles
Elevation gain: 200′
High point: 1280′
Hiking time: 3 hours
Difficulty: Moderate
USGS *Stehekin*
Green Trails *Stehekin*

Maps 1, 3

The trail starts at the Harlequin Campground. It is 3.5 miles to the Devore Creek Trail, and 4 miles to Weaver Point. Follow the Harlequin Campground Road from its junction with the Company Creek Road .2 mile. Turn right at the signed trailhead (the road continues beyond this point). This portion of the trail is for hikers only; horse access is via a road west of the airstrip.

The trail crosses streams, swamps, and ponds on interesting bridges, and also passes through occasional old grassy, meadow-like areas. The trail mood is pastoral and tranquil. This section of the trail is .6 mile long and joins the horse trail at the end of the airstrip.

The trail enters the woods south of the airstrip after crossing a creek on a footlog. There are bridges across all streams. In one place, the trail follows beside a lazy, quiet, deep, meandering side channel of the Stehekin River; this is a forest dell of substantial beauty.

At 1.5 miles, a short scramble east of the trail onto a grassy bluff offers a fine view of Rainbow Falls with the Stehekin River in the foreground. Harlequin ducks are often seen in this part of the river. Cross Devore Creek on a bridge upstream. The trail ends slightly northwest of the Weaver Point Campground. Walking time is about 1½ hours.

By prearrangement with the people at the North Cascades Lodge, it is possible to obtain boat transportation from the Weaver

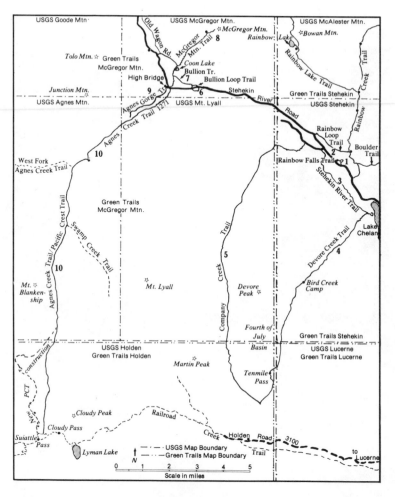

Map 1

Point Dock back to Stehekin. Otherwise, steps must be retraced.

There is ample time to make this walk, in both directions, between the morning and afternoon shuttlebus trips. This lowland trail is generally open from late March until late November. Altitude gain is negligible downstream and 200′ upstream. Watch out for yellow jackets!   (August 1979)

Rainbow Falls from Stehekin River Trail

Devore Creek Trail

Round trip: 20 miles
Elevation gain: 5400'
High point: 6500'
Hiking time: 2 days

Map 1

Difficulty: Strenuous
USGS *Stehekin, Lucerne, Holden*
Green Trails *Stehekin, Lucerne, Holden*

If possible, arrange boat transportation to the Weaver Point Dock. Go northwest through the campground to reach the powerline and pick up the trail at that point. It is .5 mile to the bridge at Devore Creek and .1 mile to the trail junction beyond the bridge. Get water when crossing Devore Creek; there is no water for the next several miles. From the junction, it is 8.5 miles to the Fourth of July Basin and 10 miles to Tenmile Pass (6500'); the lakeshore is 1100', so the elevation gain is more than a vertical mile.

After a deceptively gentle .2 mile, this trail goes up steeply. At .8 mile, there is a view of the head of the lake and of Stehekin. Enter Glacier Peak Wilderness Area at 1.2 miles. The trail switchbacks steeply and then turns west above Devore Creek. After gaining 1500' in 2.5 miles, first water is reached (the next water is over an hour away). 100 feet beyond the small creek providing second water, and 25 feet below the trail, there is a fair campsite for two tents. This is 4 miles from the trailhead.

Near the 5 mile sign, Bird Creek Camp is near the creek in the deep forest. There are many flies and no views, but it is a satisfactory stopping point otherwise. Obtaining water is not a problem beyond second water. At 6.5 miles, the path enters an avalanche meadow with the first good views. After 6 hours of hiking and 4400' gain, cross Devore Creek into Fourth of July Basin. There is a good campsite (unfortunately abused by extensive horse use) a few feet beyond Devore Creek. The first 4 miles of trail are steep and hot, but the gradient is more gradual thereafter.

Although Fourth of July Basin is pretty, it is neither level nor splendid. Flies and mosquitoes are a substantial problem.

From the campsite (the only good one in the area), the trail goes up, ducking in and out of timber alongside an avalanche meadow. The larch forest begins just above the high camp. There are a few level spots beside the trail, but there is no water and no evidence of prior occupancy. It is 1.5 miles with 1000' elevation gain to the summit of Tenmile Pass. Here are good views of Fourth of July Basin, Devore Canyon, and mountains to the west. The pass is flat on top and provides several satisfactory scenic campsites. Water can be obtained from a small creek .2 mile to the southwest. See Company Creek Trail description for details regarding travel beyond this point.

The Devore Creek Trail is not well-maintained and is muddy, rough, hazardous at slide areas, and overgrown, but not difficult to follow. An early start is advisable in order to gain altitude before the heat of the day.   (August 1979)

Company Creek Trail

5

Map 1

Round trip: 29 miles to Tenmile Pass
Elevation gain: 5500'
High point: 6700'
Hiking time: 2 days
Difficulty: Strenuous
USGS *Stehekin, Mt. Lyall, Holden*
Green Trails *Stehekin, McGregor Mtn., Holden*

Take the shuttlebus to the Company Creek Bridge, 4 miles upriver from Stehekin. Cross the bridge, and follow the road past the airfield and powerhouse. The trailhead is .1 mile beyond the powerhouse on the west (left) side of the road and is signed. From here, it is 11.5 miles to Hilgard Pass and 14.5 miles to Tenmile Pass at the head of Devore Creek. (It is possible to make a loop trip requiring 3 days out of this walk; see Devore Creek Trail.)

The Company Creek pathway begins climbing out of the valley through the forest. There are views down into the valley about 1 and 2 miles from the trailhead. At 1.9 miles is the Glacier Peak Wilderness Area boundary. There is a campsite (Cedar Camp) 3 miles from the trailhead. Fivemile Camp on the north side of the Company Creek crossing has 4 or 5 tent sites; protect food from rodents at this camp. Company Creek must be crossed at this point, either by fording or on one of several footlogs located 50 feet above the horse ford. The crossing is somewhat hazardous, particularly when the logs are wet or the creek is high.

In 1979, the trail was brushed from the trailhead to Fivemile Camp. There had been no maintenance on the remainder of the loop. Traversing overgrown trails, particularly during or after a rain, is unpleasant at best.

After crossing Company Creek, the trail contours up the hillside, coming into the Hilgard Valley after a few miles. Hilgard Creek must be forded twice, at 8 and 8.5 miles; these fords were not difficult in August, but could present problems during the high spring runoff. The meadow below Hilgard Pass is at 9.8 miles. There is a splendid camping area in the meadow at the 10 mile mark. (There are no campsites other than the three mentioned.)

From this campsite, the trail switchbacks steeply to Hilgard Pass 1 mile beyond. Hilgard Pass is at 6500' and the total altitude gain is 5250'. The average walking time to the pass is about 9 hours, with the descent taking about 5 hours. Obtaining water is not a problem.

From Hilgard Pass, the trail drops downward less steeply, losing 1200' in 1.5 miles to reach the Tenmile Basin meadow. This area is splendid and offers opportunities for cross-country side trips in various directions. There is a waterfall coming from Martin Peak to the northwest. Below the meadow, the trail goes into forest. An unsigned and difficult to locate scrabble trail drops through the meadow to the west (right) of the creek and follows the creek down to Holden Village, 3 miles away. This trail is not on the map and is recommended only for those experienced in cross-country wilderness travel.

The formal Tenmile Basin Trail runs fairly level for 1 mile and then turns east and begins the steep ascent to Tenmile Pass. There is a good campsite in a meadow 1 mile below the pass. Tenmile Pass is flat and is also a good campsite; obtain water from a small creek .2 mile to the southwest. Devore Creek Trail leads from Tenmile Pass back to Lake Chelan.

There are larch trees at both passes. These trees are scenicly spectacular each fall when their needles turn golden yellow and glow in the sunlight; the show lasts from about September 20 to October 10. Berry picking is good in the meadows in the early fall.

(August 1979)

Bullion Loop

6

Round trip: 1.7 miles
Elevation gain: 200'
High point: 1600'
Hiking time: 45 minutes
Difficulty: Moderately easy
USGS *McGregor Mtn.*
Green Trails *McGregor Mtn.*

Map 1

This loop footpath begins at Bullion Camp, 1.5 miles up river from the Courtney Ranch. The walking time for the loop is about 45 minutes, with an altitude gain of 200'. If one starts at the most downriver point and walks away from the river, in .1 mile, a trail junction is reached; the right trail leads to Cascade Corrals (Courtney Ranch). The Bullion Trail turns left. .2 mile beyond, a small creek is crossed on a footlog, and .4 mile further, another creek is passed. A few feet from this point is the junction with the Coon Lake/Old Wagon Road Trail (see trip #7). From the junction, it is .15 mile to Bullion Camp and .25 mile from Bullion Camp to Stehekin Road. (There is also a short way-trail from the camp to the road.)

Cross the road and follow the trail .1 mile to the river. From here, it is .3 mile back to the point of beginning. Unfortunately, Bullion Camp is not scenic. The most pleasant areas are in the maple forest, and the short stretch alongside of the Stehekin River. The total distance is about 1.7 miles. Watch out for rattlesnakes!

(August, 1979)

Coon Lake via Old Wagon Road

7

Round trip: 3.2 miles
Elevation gain: 700'
High point: 2300'
Hiking time: 1½ hours
Difficulty: Moderate
USGS *McGregor Mtn.*
Green Trails *McGregor Mtn.*

Map 1

If you follow the upper portion of the Bullion Loop Trail (see trip #6), you will be on the Old Wagon Road which ran from the shore of Lake Chelan to the Black Warrior Mine in Horseshoe Basin. This road bypasses the two bridges over the river (High Bridge and Tumwater).

From the junction with the Bullion Loop Trail, it is .2 mile to a section where the road crosses talus slope with a good view of Agnes Mountain to the southwest. At 1 mile, the road joins the McGregor Mountain Trail from High Bridge to Coon Lake. Half a mile further, there is another good view up the Agnes Valley to Agnes Mountain. Coon Lake is .1 mile beyond this viewpoint.

A few yards beyond the lake is the junction with the McGregor Mountain Trail or one can continue on the Wagon Road to reach the Stehekin Road above High Bridge 1 mile further. This trail is a more scenic, although slightly longer, approach to Coon Lake than the trail from High Bridge. On either trail, watch out for rattlesnakes! For a description of Coon Lake, see McGregor Mountain.

The trail following the old Wagon Road continues northwest from its junction with the Stehekin Road above Tumwater Bridge, and parallels the Stehekin Road for 3 miles. This trail is in woods throughout, and rejoins the Stehekin Road .1 mile before Bridge Creek Camp. This section of the trail provides an alternative to the Stehekin Road for walking between the Agnes Creek and Bridge Creek sections of the Pacific Crest Trail.   (August, 1979)

McGregor Mountain Trail

8

Round trip: 16 miles (summit); 14 miles (Heaton Camp)
Elevation gain: 6500' (summit); 5200' (Heaton Camp)   **Maps 1, 2**
High point: 8100'
Hiking time: 2 days
Difficulty: Strenuous
USGS *McGregor Mountain (trail not shown)*
Green Trails *McGregor Mountain*

The trail starts at the ranger cabin at High Bridge on the Stehekin Road 10.5 miles from Stehekin. Switchbacks start almost immediately. .6 mile from the trailhead, there is a signed junction as the old Stehekin Wagon Road joins the trail from the right. A 30 minute walk with 550' gain brings one to Coon Lake, 1.2 miles from the trailhead. Agnes Mountain can be seen at two or three places along the trail to the lake. Coon Lake could be described as either a deep swamp or shallow lake; it does not contain fish, and is not particularly scenic. Beaver frequent the area; it is also a good viewing area for observing water fowl, particularly in the spring when several species of ducks are engaged in mating rituals.

The trail continues to the northwest end of the lake, where there is a signed junction. From here, the old Wagon Road continues 1 mile to its junction with the Stehekin Road above the Tumwater Bridge, and then 3 additional miles, almost to the Bridge Creek Campground. The trail to McGregor Mountain turns east, drops down slightly, and follows the north side of the lake; seemingly unending switchbacks are then encountered as the trail begins its climb from the east side of the lake.

1 mile from the Coon Lake junction, the trail passes a waterfall on the right. One can obtain water via a steep scrabble trail at this point. Drink deeply, and fill canteens since the next easily accessible water is several miles away. Just below this waterfall is a bluff with views of Coon Lake below and the Agnes Valley to the west; day hikers may find this point an attractive place for eating lunch.

From the end of Coon Lake, the trail switchbacks remorselessly, initially in ponderosa pine forest. At about 3.5 miles, there is another bluff for sitting and viewing; Coon Lake is appreciably smaller now below. More mountains are visible, including Dome, Boston, Goode and Buckner. The forest is left behind and the trail passes through the Canadian or Douglas fir zone. Between miles 4 and 5, scrabbles over rather difficult terrain allow one to reach water at several locations if desperate, but the first easy water is available at 5.5 miles where it can be obtained a few feet to the

(McGregor Mountain)

right of the trail. At 6 miles, an unofficial campsite is located below the trail, with water from a stream nearby. The first larch trees are at about this point, which marks the transition to the Hudsonian or alpine fir zone. At 6.3 miles, the trail, which has been going up a fairly open valley for the past 2 miles, suddenly enters a talus bowl; there is one tent site at this point without obvious water.

After switchbacking up through the talus bowl, Heaton Camp, located at a cliff on the left (north side) of the talus bowl, is reached. Look carefully for the 150' side trail to the left (west). There is a sign in 100', but none at the junction. This is the only designated camping area and is at about 7000'.

Heaton Camp has two fire pits, a moderate wood supply, a toilet 300' to the north behind a granite outcrop, water from a small spring 100' below and northwest of the camp, and water from a larger spring .1 mile down the trail. Water from this source can be sporadic. There are six to eight small tent sites. The area is almost bug-free. There is evidence of horses throughout most of the camp area.

Note an interesting, faint trail up the ridge to the southeast; this was probably made by mountain goats. The view from the campsite to the west is splendid, but views to the south and north are limited by ridges and, of course, the main bulk of McGregor is to the east.

An additional fairly steep .4 mile trail leads to the base of the talus slope beneath the summit of the peak. Here are two standing timbers of the A frame used to winch materials for the lookout from this point to the summit. The summit can be identified by the radio aerial of the Park Service repeater station clearly visible from below.

From this point, the route to the summit looks formidable. However, if the proper route is located and followed, the ascent, though exposed, is not technical (Class 2). From the base of the talus slope, the best route is between two large rocks near the top of the rocky incline; both are marked with hard-to-spot red paint (a cairn was built on the left rock in 1980). Continue to the end of the highest left talus slope. Turn right at this point, and follow a ledge approximately 200' to the gully on the right (look for red marker arrows). Just before reaching the gully, turn left and go above a 20' rock block in the chute above the original talus slope. From here, the route is more obvious and better marked. It goes up the ridge to the left, and near the top cuts right and goes through a notch to the left of the first tor left of the summit. From here, there are magnificent views of peaks to the north and east. Cross snow, or talus later in the year, on a faint trail east of this spire, and then proceed upward on trail, snow, or talus 150 yards to the summit. Red arrows and dots are helpful route markers, but at times are not easily seen. There is no other simple, safe route to the summit; it is most important not to go to the right at the base of the talus slope!

The flat 10' x 12' summit block was the site of the old McGregor Lookout. Even today, metal, fused glass, and other remnants of this structure can be found. Twenty feet below is the solar powered Park Service repeater station and aerial.

From the summit, views in every direction provide a panorama of practically every significant peak in the North Cascades, except Baker and Shuksan, which are obscured by peaks to the northwest. Immediately below is the ice and snow of the Sandalee Glacier. The whole Stehekin Valley is spread out below, and Lake Chelan curves out of sight near Round and Domke Mountains. The hiker is now in the arctic-alpine zone, where only shrubs and flowers flourish briefly during the summer.

Almost anyone will reluctantly leave this splendid viewpoint. Descent, although easier on the lungs, is at best only a little faster since one missed step could have severe consequences.

On the way down, less heavily laden and less fatigued, one can perhaps appreciate the creek flowers more than when coming up, and be more sensitive to the life zone changes. Only 35 minutes of walking separate the last larch (at about 5.5 miles) from the first ponderosa pine (at about 4 miles from High Bridge).

Allow 5 hours up fully packed to Heaton Camp. Round trip from Heaton Camp to the summit takes another 2½ hours. It is 3 hours down to the trailhead from Heaton Camp.

Watch for rattlesnakes on the lower portions of the trail. An early start is advisable to avoid the heat of the day while still at low altitude. One quart of water is mandatory; an extra quart and several salt tablets are advisable.

This trail is without question strenuous even to Heaton Camp; however if pursued to the summit, this is probably the most scenic and splendid trail in the Stehekin area. Experienced climbers with appropriate equipment can continue cross-country over ice and rock from the summit to Rainbow Lake; this mountaineering traverse takes about 8 hours.   (August 1980)

Agnes Gorge Trail

9

Round trip: 5 miles
Elevation gain: 300'
High point: 2000'
Hiking time: 2 hours
Difficulty: Moderately easy
USGS *McGregor Mtn., Mt. Lyall, Agnes Mtn.*
Green Trails *McGregor Mtn.*

Map 1

The trailhead is .2 mile above High Bridge and .1 mile beyond the Pacific Crest trailhead. The trailhead is signed. There are nice views of McGregor Peak to the east from the first portion of the trail, and a spectacular view of Agnes Mountain to the west at about 2 miles. Wildflowers are impressive as are blooming dogwoods in season. Trail distance is 2.5 miles to the gorge; walking time is approximately one hour in each direction and elevation gain is minimal either way.

The trail enters the Glacier Peak Wilderness and leaves the National Park at 1.3 miles. Just beyond 2 miles, there is a very impressive view of the Agnes River running swiftly below. There are many wildflowers in this area. Just before the end of the trail, multiple trilliums bloom in late May, and an occasional calypso orchid can be found.

The main trail terminates at the chasm of Agnes Gorge. Thirty years ago, the Forest Service had a suspension bridge at this location which gradually became hazardous due to heavy winter snowfall, and eventually was destroyed. An old metal chair seat from the bridge is still there.

For the hiker, stay on a way trail leaving the main trail a few feet before the gorge, and follow it .1 mile west and down. The head of the gorge can be reached with reasonable safety in this manner, and it is possible with care to climb a great pile of driftwood, and actually stand on top of the precipice above the major falls within the gorge. The place is hypnotically beautiful. A waterfall coming from the south side makes the area even more impressive. There is a good campsite for 2 tents here. Note the footlog across the creek above the cataract. It would probably be possible to·inch across with reasonable safety. A fall here, however, might well be fatal if one were swept into the torrent below. Great care should be exercised in this area.

It would probably be possible to reach this area also via the Agnes Creek/Pacific Crest Trail which would give access to the south side of the gorge.

This is a splendid trail for mountain views, wildflowers, views of the river and the impressive chasm and cataracts. There are reasonable amounts of water enroute (at least in late May), but no other obvious campsites.

Beware of ticks; use repellant and check each other after coming off the trail.   (May 1978)

Agnes Creek (Pacific Crest Trail)

10

Round trip: 35 miles
Elevation gain: 4400'
High point: 5983' (Suiattle Pass)
Hiking time: 3-4 days
Difficulty: Moderately strenuous
USGS *McGregor Mtn., Mt. Lyall, Agnes Mtn., Holden*
Green Trails *McGregor Mtn., Holden*

Map 1

Just beyond High Bridge on the Stehekin Road (10.5 miles from Stehekin) is the Agnes Creek trailhead at 1600'. The trailhead is easily reached by a very short walk from the High Bridge Guard Station.

After .1 mile, the trail crosses Agnes Creek on a sturdy bridge and then begins a gradual climb through the deep woods to Suiattle Pass, 17 long miles away. At 2 miles, the trail passes near the brink of Agnes Gorge. Cross Trapper Creek at 3.8 miles. At 4.9 miles is the junction with the West Fork of Agnes Creek Trail. There are good campsites at Fivemile Creek, .1 mile east of the junction above the west bank of Pass Creek. At 7.9 miles is the junction with the Swamp Creek Trail and Swamp Creek Camp at 2780'. Cedar Camp (sometimes known as Spruce Creek Camp) is at 9.2 miles, and Hemlock Camp with benches, table, and fire ring is at 11.9 miles (3560').

Cross Glacier Creek at 12.1 miles. Near the end of the forest at 13.5 miles and 3850' is an unnamed campsite. At 14.9 miles and 4400', leave the forest and enter a large, bushy meadow. At 16.6 miles, there is a good campsite with table, firepit and toilet, and .1 mile beyond the campsite is the junction with the trail to Cloudy Pass. Railroad Creek Trail from Holden also joins Agnes Creek Trail at this point. Suiattle Pass is .4 mile beyond at 5983'. The trail from Hemlock Camp to Suiattle Pass will be rerouted higher and to the west in 1981.

This long valley walk is probably the least enjoyable portion of the Pacific Crest Trail between Manning Park and Stevens Pass. There are few views until the last 2 miles of this trail. There is no shortage of wood or water enroute. The lower portions of the trail open in April and remain open into November. The high country is open from about July 15 to October 15. A backpacker in above average physical condition will require one long, hard day to go from the Stehekin Road to Suiattle Pass (17 miles and 4400′ gain); most hikers will take 1½ to 2 days to make the ascent, although the descent can be done fairly easily in 7 hours, even allowing for lunch and rest stops.

Cascade Pass

11

Round trip: 10 miles
Elevation gain: 2650′   **Map 2**
High point: 5400′
Hiking time: 5 hours
Difficulty: Moderately strenuous
USGS *Goode Mtn., Cascade Pass*
Green Trails *McGregor Mtn., Cascade Pass*

The trailhead begins at Cottonwood Camp at the end of the Stehekin Road. The trail initially ascends gradually along the Stehekin River, detouring upward briefly to avoid the avalanche debris from the cliffs to the south, which dammed the Stehekin River and obliterated the old trail in the 1970s. It is 1 mile to Basin Creek Camp, where there are 5 or 6 established, scattered campsites. A bear cable has been placed in this area to help campers preserve food supplies from marauding bruins.

Cross Basin Creek on a high plank bridge. The trail climbs more steeply from this point, switchbacking on the Mine to Market Road toward Horseshoe Basin (see separate description). The trail to Cascade Pass forks left after several switchbacks and traverses gradually upward to cross the waterfall of Doubtful Creek 1 mile beyond. Above this point, there are 13 switchbacks ending in the woods above Pelton Basin. The trail then goes fairly level through timber for .4 mile, and breaks out into open country, crossing a talus slope and then switchbacking to reach Cascade Pass 5 miles from the start of the trail.

The altitude at Cottonwood is 2750′; Cascade Pass is 5400′. With ups and downs, figure almost 3000′ gain. Up-time: 3 hours; down-time: 1¾ hours. Lots of water along the way. Watch for pica and marmots; they are enjoyable animals to observe!

Cascade Pass can also be reached by a 4 mile trail from the west. To reach the trail, drive the North Cascades Highway (Highway 20) to Marblemount. Cross the Skagit River and follow the road to its end (the last 2 miles is rough road). The trail begins in the parking lot at road end.

The Cascade Pass area is one of the most spectacular in the North Cascades. One never tires of the walk, no matter how many times it has been done. If you have only a short time to spend in

Magic Mountain

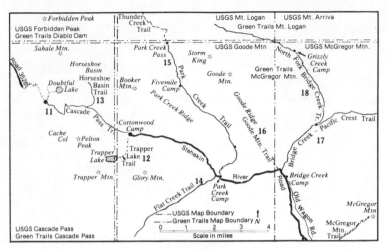

NOTE: No shuttlebus is scheduled above High Bridge in 1981 due to road washout. Check with Ranger for availability.

Map 2

the Valley, this is the primary walk for which you should strive. Moderately strong hikers can day hike this route between the first and last shuttlebuses of the day. For more leisurely exploration, plan to spend the night at Basin Creek Camp or (less desirably) at Cottonwood.

Active and aggressive attempts to replant damaged areas at Cascade Pass continue. A greenhouse for growing high alpine plants has been constructed at the Marblemount Ranger Station. Green netting has been placed in many areas of the pass in an effort to retain seeds and support plant growth; it is important not to walk on any areas where netting is visible.

In 1981, a designated campsite for hikers will be established in the timber near Pelton Basin, one mile east of the pass.

(August 1980)

DOUBTFUL LAKE

Just before Cascade Pass is reached, the side trail to Doubtful Lake and Sahale Arm goes to the right (north). This steeper secondary footpath then switchbacks up Sahale Arm, gaining 1000′ in .7 mile. At the top of the arm, descend the steep north side of the arm and lose about 1000′ to reach Doubtful Lake. Note the evidence of the mining activity that took place here in the late 1800s.

Fishing is generally good, although the lake is rather heavily

Doubtful Lake waterfall

fished in the summer. The scenery features magnificent views of Sahale to the north and McGregor to the east. Total distance from the pass is 1.5 miles.

Camping is no longer allowed anywhere in the Cascade Pass area. This day-use only policy is necessary to preserve the fragile high mountain environment. Please stay on the trails, and treat this splendid area gently.

SAHALE ARM

Instead of descending to Doubtful Lake, it is possible to continue in Sahale Arm meadows by following the mountaineer's scrabble trail to an elevation of 8000'. At this point it is necessary to traverse a glacier and those without experience in climbing should turn back. Sahale Arm features spectacular views of the surrounding "sea of peaks".

CACHE COL

It is also possible to follow a mountaineer's trail beginning at the pass and traversing upward to the southeast across steep snow and talus slopes to a promontory .5 mile above the pass. This is a dangerous trail and should be attempted only by those experienced in climbing techniques. From this promontory, descend onto snow and ice, and then contour up over the glacier to reach Cache Col to the southeast.

Just above this col, there is a spectacular but exposed campsite from which to watch the mere mortals below. There is also camping 1 mile further at Kool-Aid Lake, 1000' lower. Basic snow and ice climbing training are required to reach the col safely.

TRAPPER LAKE

To reach Trapper Lake from the pass, descend on the trail to Lake Chelan .5 mile. Take the lower (right) fork of the trail and descend into Pelton Basin, crossing to the south side of the creek. Ascend a moderately apparent scrabble path at the southeast side of Pelton Basin, gaining about 500' to a very nice camping area overlooking the Stehekin Valley. From here, two traverses over scrabble trail lead to the ridge overlooking Trapper Lake after an additional walk of 1 mile. A steep descent of .2 mile (easy early in the season when snow is present, but a difficult bushwhack late in the season) will bring one to the west end of Trapper Lake. Fishing and campsites are available at the lake.

Trapper Lake Trail (East End) from Cottonwood Camp

12

Round trip: 1.5 miles
Elevation gain: 1400'
High point: 4165'
Hiking time: 5 hours
Difficulty: Strenuous
USGS *Goode Mtn., Cascade Pass*
Green Trails *McGregor Mtn., Cascade Pass*

Map 2

Trapper Lake near Cascade Pass

This is a strenuous cross-country route for experienced hikers only! The distance is .7 mile as the crow flies with an elevation gain of 1400′. The hiking time up is 2 hours if lightly-packed; allow 3 hours with a heavy pack.

Cross the Stehekin River on a log in one of the Cottonwood Campgrounds, and go up the valley in the trees to where the trees cross over to the south side of the valley. Aim for the base of the talus slope beneath the prominent cliff. Climb the talus slope to the base of the rock bluff. Go east around the base of the bluff until reaching a small chute; follow this to the timber.

From here, there is no route-finding problem to the lake. There is a campsite located near the lake outlet. Watch carefully as you ascend so you can find the same route on descent. Other routes are more difficult and/or dangerous.

For information on reaching the west end of Trapper Lake from the Pelton Basin area, see the description for Cascade Pass.

Horseshoe Basin Trail

13

Round trip: 3 miles
Elevation gain: 1150'   **Map 2**
High point: 4800'
Hiking time: 1½ hours from the junction; 4 hours from
    Cottonwood Camp
Difficulty: Moderate
USGS *Cascade Pass*
Green Trails *Cascade Pass*

Horseshoe Basin can be reached by continuing on the
abandoned Mine to Market Road (now a trail) 2 miles west of
Cottonwood Camp, or 3 miles east of Cascade Pass. (This is a less
rigorous one day trip from the Cottonwood trailhead than the trip
to Cascade Pass; although not as scenic, it is an enjoyable
alternative for hikers physically unable to make the trip to the pass
between the first and last shuttlebuses of the day.)

Gain 1150' in 1.5 miles to the large cirque between Sahale,
Boston, Ripsaw Ridge and Buckner Mountains. Note the many
active waterfalls cascading down from the snow and ice fields
above. The trail now ends at the Black Warrior Mine, easily
located by the extensive tailings below the mine shaft entrance.

During most of the summer, there is a snow field just below the
mine which may present problems to the inexperienced; use
considerable caution in this area. If in doubt, go down about
2 switchbacks, cross the snow field at that point, and work your
way back up the talus slope, staying to the right of the creek and to
the left of the mine tailings.

This mine is now in the National Register of Historical Places; it
has been restored by the Park Service, and is safe to enter and
explore. Carry at least 2 flashlights. Watch both your head and
your feet. The shaft in places is only 5 feet high, and in addition,
there are pipes and rough areas over which one could easily trip.
At the mine entrance, notice the stove, hot water tank, and room
just inside the mine shaft which presumably served as a warming
and cooking area. Allow eyes to adjust to the darkness. The shaft
penetrates the mountain perhaps 150', and then the main shaft
turns left an additional 75'; further penetration is felt unsafe by
the Park Service, and there is a screen prohibiting more
exploration at this point.

Although there is lumber and other debris outside of the mine,
there are no standing cabins since winter avalanches have
decimated the area with regularity. Wildflowers are profuse,
particularly mimulus, along the trail. The jagged "sawteeth" of
Ripsaw Ridge above are also impressive. The area is designated

for day-use only; the nearest camp is at Basin Creek, 2.3 miles away. The trail has been brushed and is in good condition, although parts are muddy and follow a stream bed. There is no problem obtaining water in the basin.

Near the junction with the Cascade Pass Trail, there is a splendid proliferation of succulent yellow blooming rock plants (sedum or stonecrop) along the trail in late July.

Before leaving this area, let your imagination go back to the winter of 1909, when miners wintered over here, going between cabin and mine shaft through tunnels dug underneath the 30-foot snow pack. (July 1980)

Flat Creek Trail

14

Map 2

Round trip: 6.6 miles
Elevation gain: 500'
High point: 2800'
Hiking time: 3 hours
Difficulty: Moderate
USGS *Goode Mtn.*
Green Trails *McGregor Mtn.*

Flat Creek Trail starts on the Stehekin Road and is 3.3 miles long. 50 yards from the road, the trail crosses the Stehekin River on a well-built bridge. This is a splendid picnic spot since the river chasm is spectacularly beautiful, particularly in August when there are two different kinds of wildflowers growing out of the rock on the west side.

The trail goes intermittently through forest; in places one can look up the valley to the crest peaks of Ptarmigan Traverse and to lesser peaks on the left side of the valley. At 3.1 miles, the trail divides with the right fork being the horse crossing and the left fork leading to a potentially difficult footlog crossing. .2 mile beyond, the trail ends abruptly in dense slide alder.

No obvious campsites were seen, although it would be possible to camp in the last .3 mile near Flat Creek. The "good campsite" mentioned in the Park Service's Stehekin trail information sheet could not be located.

The round trip can be accomplished between shuttlebus runs. The altitude gain is about 500' in, and 200' returning. Check with the ranger to see if the trail has been brushed. If overgrown, it could be unpleasant, particularly during or after rain.

A recent rockslide off a major peak to the left of the trail going in is impressive. Water is available at 1 mile where there is a series of puncheon, at Flat Creek, and at the Stehekin River.

(August 1978)

Park Creek Pass Trail

15

Round trip: 16 miles
Elevation gain: 3800'   **Map 2**
High point: 6140'
Hiking time: 8 hours
Difficulty: Moderately strenuous
USGS *Goode Mtn.*
Green Trails *McGregor Mtn.*

Take the shuttlebus (or walk) 18 miles up the road from
Stehekin, or 4.5 miles down the road from Cottonwood Camp to the
trailhead. An unobtrusive sign is located where the trail takes off
north of the road; there is an unimproved camping area near the
creek to the right of the start of the trail.

After 100 yards, the trail goes moderately steeply upward. At
1 mile, there is a viewpoint and a small spring from which water
can be obtained. .1 mile beyond, a 50 foot walk to the right to a
rocky knob permits splendid views up the Flat Creek Valley.
100 yards or so beyond this viewpoint, the trail "tops out", and
there are again views over the Stehekin Valley from a rock a few
feet to the right of the trail.

From this point, the trail drops gently downward to reach
Twomile Camp. Hiking time to the camp, fully-packed, is 1 hour
from the trailhead. There is a toilet on the hillside above the camp,
and there is space for about 3 tents crowded rather closely together
adjacent to Park Creek.

The trail forks at this point, with the horse trail going left. The
hiker trail crosses a sturdy bridge to the north side of Park Creek.
The trail then goes sharply up for several hundred yards and
gradually upward thereafter. Fully-packed, it takes an additional
1½ hours to reach Fivemile Camp. There are good views in the
open areas and water is available at the 4 mile mark.

Most of Fivemile Camp is in timber without views, but Campsite
#4, 50 yards beyond, is splendidly located in open meadow with a
spectacular view of the great cirque beneath Booker and Buckner
Mountains. Wood is scarce. Water is available from a small
creek. Bear cable is available, but without stringers.

From Fivemile Camp to Park Creek Pass takes about 1½ hours,
lightly-packed. The trail first goes through the brushy valley floor
for .5 mile, then goes up the hillside, crosses a stream, and at
7 miles, breaks out into meadow. After it leaves the valley floor, it
goes steeply upward. It is a long 8 miles to the .2 mile long pass,
which is snow-filled at the bottom.

The trail contours above and on the northeast side of the pass.
Views down Thunder Creek from the place where the snow
abruptly terminates on the north side of the pass are quite

spectacular. Camping is prohibited at the pass itself. Further to the west on the high ridge approach to Mt. Buckner, "legal" camping for mountaineers is allowed. Grouse, marmots, and pica inhabit the area. The down-time from the pass to Fivemile Camp is slightly more than an hour, and from Fivemile Camp to Stehekin Road is about 2 hours. There is adequate water between Fivemile Camp and the pass. Legal camping must be 1 mile off the trail for 3 miles on either side of the crest of Park Creek Pass.

The trailhead is at 2340'. There is 1000' gain in the first 1.5 miles. Twomile Camp is at 3500'; Fivemile Camp is at 4100'. Park Creek Pass is 6140'; Buckner Mountain is 9112'. Storm King Mountain can be seen from the trail 4 miles from the Stehekin Road. Beyond the pass, the trail follows Thunder Creek north 20 miles to the North Cascades Highway and Colonial Creek Campground.

The pass area is really splendid and relatively isolated and uncrowded. It is possible to travel cross-country into the cirque beneath Buckner Mountain, or to go higher on the mountain for ever-improving views.   (August 1978)

Goode Ridge Trail

16

Round trip: 11 miles
Elevation gain: 4600'
High point: 6760'
Hiking time: full day
Difficulty: Strenuous
USGS *Goode Mountain, McGregor Mountain*
Green Trails *McGregor Mountain*

Map 2

The unsigned trailhead is 16.5 miles from Stehekin, .1 mile beyond the Bridge Creek Bridge. The initial few feet of tread are fairly apparent, but after that the trail is difficult to locate for the next 200'. Go west 50', then northwest to the left of a dead tree, and at about 200', the path becomes relatively obvious. Look for flagging tape if the route is unclear.

This trail was abandoned for a number of years, but was worked by a trail crew in 1980, and major impediments to passage were removed; however, the trail is still considered a scrabble trail for its entire length. In a few places, the tread is difficult to locate. Cut log ends may also assist in route-finding.

Before starting up, drop below the road to Bridge Creek and drink deeply from the two splendid pools just below the trailhead; also fill water bottles at this point. It is 1.5 miles, and about 45 minutes hiking time, to a small spring where more water may be obtained. Beyond there is no water until snow patches near or at the high point are reached; after mid-August in an average year, little or no snow will be present. Two full water bottles are therefore recommended in the late summer and early fall.

The trail goes up steeply and remorselessly in woods with few views for the first 2.5 miles (allow 1½ hours hiking time, moderately packed). The trail then breaks out of the forest and there is a fine view of Bridge Creek. Views improve progressively as one gains further altitude. At 3.8 miles (50 minutes later), the trail re-enters woods for .3 mile; there are two campsites in this area: one dry and one near a small snow patch.

The trail again comes out of the timber and goes north to the east side of Goode Ridge. It then switchbacks and contours south to the south side of the ridge. Between 5.2 and 5.3 miles, there are multiple campsites with water available from snow fields. Beside the trail, there is a very scenic, almost dead, white bark pine leaning on top of a large granite boulder with blooming heather beneath.

The top, at 5.5 miles, is level, and there are many good campsites along the summit ridge with water available from patchy snow. Green View Lake can be seen to the northwest nestled between Memaloose and Goode ridges. There are wild-flowers beyond the 2.5 mile point. From the top, one can also see Goode Mountain, Booker Mountain, Trapper Lake, Glory Mountain, Tolo Mountain, McGregor Peak, Flat Creek, a portion of the Ptarmigan Traverse, Dome Peak, Glacier Peak, and the Stehekin, Bridge and Dead Man Creek Valleys. It is truly a spectacular 360 degree panorama!

At the high point, the rock platform, cables, glass, and metal mark the site of the fire lookout destroyed by the Forest Service in the early 1950s.   (July 1980)

Bridge Creek (Pacific Crest Trail)

17

One way: 12.2 miles
Elevation gain: 2300' from Stehekin Road
        to North Cascades Highway
High point: 4400'
Hiking time: 6 hours
Difficulty: Moderately strenuous
USGS *McGregor Mtn., McAlester Mtn., Washington Pass*
Green Trails *McGregor Mtn., Stehekin, Washington Pass*

Maps 2, 3

At the present time, this 12.2 mile trail is a section of the Pacific Crest Trail. From the valley, the trailhead is .2 mile before the Bridge Creek Bridge. The trail ascends through deep forest, gains a moderate amount of altitude, and then drops to a well-constructed bridge over Bridge Creek. From here it switchbacks up, gaining 400' to reach the junction with the North Fork Trail at 3 miles. The North Fork Camp is at the junction of Bridge Creek with the North Fork; there are good campsites here for 15 people beside the rushing water. There is a scenic campsite .2 mile before Maple Creek for no more than 4 people on a rocky shelf above the gorge; this is the prettiest camp on the entire trail, but requires obtaining water from Maple Creek and is also an exposed site in inclement weather.

Cross Maple Creek on a bridge 50 feet above the site of the old ford. The access trails to the bridge on either side may not be apparent; however, the bridge can easily be seen from either direction as one approaches the creek. Sixmile Camp is indeed at 6 miles. The trail to this camp goes down to the river, where there are a number of campsites beneath the trees. Mud is a problem here in wet weather.

For better campsites, continue .8 mile to South Fork Camp. There are several very nice campsites by Bridge Creek. A footlog permits access to Rainbow Lake 6 miles away. (See Rainbow Lake Trail for description.) At 8.5 miles, Hideaway Camp (on Bridge Creek) is recommended as a bivouac site only. A bridge crossing .5 mile further allows access to Fireweed Camp on the other side of Bridge Creek. Here is the junction to the trails to Twisp Pass, McAlester Pass, Stiletto Meadows and Peak, and Copper Pass. In another .8 mile is a campsite and an old cabin belonging to the Bridge Creek Mines. The cabin could provide emergency shelter for 6 to 12 persons. Plastic helps keep the roof from leaking.

At 10.8 miles is the north border of the National Park. Cross Bridge Creek at 11 miles on a footlog downstream from the horse ford. .1 mile up from the ford was the Crocker Cabin, an old mine site; remnants of mining activity are apparent in the surrounding area. Just above Crocker Cabin is the spur trail to Copper Pass and the Stiletto Meadow bypass trail. From this point, it is 1 mile to the North Cascades Highway and 2 miles to Rainy Pass.

A substantial portion of the Bridge Creek Trail is in deep forest, particularly at each end of the trail. In between, it passes through a number of avalanche slopes and open areas where views are possible. In season, there are flowers (particularly lupine and Indian paintbrush) along the route. The trail is muddy in places, but well-maintained throughout. The down-time from the highway to the Stehekin Road is about 5 hours. The up-time is 6 hours. The altitude gain from the Stehekin Road to the highway is 2300'. Wood supplies are adequate at all campsites. Water is not a problem. Bird songs speed your way along the trail. There are often many butterflies in the area.

If walking in from the North Cascades Highway, park your car

(Bridge Creek)

at the lowest portion of the highway between Rainy and Washington Passes; this will save 1 mile of deep woods walking by taking the 100 foot way trail from the road to reach the Pacific Crest Trail at this point.

Of the two access routes to the valley from the west, the Cascade Pass route is preferable to Bridge Creek since it is shorter and more scenic.   (July 1977)

North Fork of Bridge Creek

18

Round trip: 14 miles
Elevation gain: 1400'
High point: 4200'
Hiking time: One day (from junction with Bridge Creek Trail)
Difficulty: Moderate
USGS *Mt. Logan, McGregor Mtn., Goode Mtn.*
Green Trails *McGregor Mtn., Mt. Logan*

Map 2

The trail begins 3 miles up Bridge Creek from the Stehekin Road; it is located on top of a bluff .4 mile beyond the Bridge Creek Bridge and North Fork hiker's camp. The junction is at 2800' and was signed "Walker Park - 2; Trail end - 7" in August 1980.

At .2 mile, there is a view of an unnamed, three-knobbed peak at the end of Fisher Creek Valley; this mountain is 7112' high.

Many of the trees in the area are dead or dying, ostensibly from insect infestation (spruce budworm). At .8 mile, a small pond with lily pads can be seen below to the left of the trail; simultaneously, there is a view of the mountains at the head of the North Fork Valley. Water is available at 1 mile. At 1.9 miles, there is an excellent view of Goode Mountain to the south.

The trail enters Walker Park at 2.1 miles; here is another excellent view of Goode, and of the waterfall cascading down its flanks. Water is available at this point. This open area, about .3 mile wide, is clearly the creation of the massive avalanches that cascade down the north face of Goode in the winter. The avalanches reach far enough up on the north side of the valley to decimate any tree growth, thus leaving an open area at a much lower elevation that is usual on valley floors in the Stehekin area.

At 2.2 miles and 3100', the Walker Park Camp is reached. It has a table, fire pit, multiple campsites, and water 100' further along the North Fork Trail. This is a horse camp, and there are lots of flies on hot days.

Beyond, the trail gently ascends through forest to Grizzly Creek Camp (3150'), 3 miles from the trailhead. Here there are 3 tent sites with metal devices in the fire pits. Forest cover precludes views from all sites. A wilderness toilet is located 100' to the left of the main trail near the campsites.

The trail crosses Grizzly Creek at a horse ford 150' beyond the campsites. In 1980, hikers could cross by following the river 200' downstream to a crude log bridge. If Grizzly Creek cannot be crossed on a downed tree, the creek must be forded. In August, this is unpleasant but not particularly dangerous provided that a proper site is selected. During spring high water, however, this ford could be hazardous; caution is suggested for those planning to go beyond Grizzly Camp in May or June.

200' feet upstream from the crossing is a fourth tent site on the bank of Grizzly Creek. This site does have a good view of the peaks at the head of the valley and a fire pit. Grizzly Creek is very noisy as it tumbles past the campsite. It is also very difficult to find a good location to hang food bags and packs in or around this campsite to protect them from animals, but the Park Service ranger advises that bear problems at this campsite have been negligible in the past.

It is best to check with the Park staff to be sure that the trail has been brushed before proceeding further. Substantial portions of the trail for the next 2 miles are in dense, tall brush, and the going could be uncomfortable in dry weather (miserable if wet) if the trail has not received its annual maintenance and brushing prior to use.

At 3.5 miles, views improve, and shortly after, water is available from a creek crossing the trail. At 4 miles, there is a good view of Goode and Storm King Mountains, and of the Goode and Wyeth hanging glaciers clinging to their flanks. Watch for nettles in the brushy areas.

At 4.1 miles, a 40' flooded area in the trail must be bypassed. A few feet further, there is a pretty, unofficial campsite to the left of the trail. At 4.3 miles, there is an open area where one can rest on scattered granite bolders, and enjoy the scenery. Water can be obtained from the North Fork of Bridge Creek, although there is a bit of glacial flour in the water. There is a waterfall at 4.6 miles, which is better heard than seen since it is obscured by brush surrounding the trail.

At 6.2 miles, a timbered ridge descends from above and there are occasional level areas. Most of the brush has disappeared and the area is grassy meadow. At 6.8 miles, the meadow is splendid. Note the twin waterfalls cascading off the unnamed mountain ahead. The tread becomes vague at 6.9 miles. At 7 miles (4200'), the trail turns a corner, permitting vistas to the north. Mt. Logan and the Douglas Glacier can be seen clearly. A wide splendid pass

(North Fork of Bridge Creek)

with a waterfall cascading hundreds of feet down the center of it is framed on the left by Mt. Logan and its hanging glaciers, and on the right by an unnamed rock spire. In the foreground is a tumultuous waterfall formed by the North Fork of Bridge Creek cascading down from the pass above. There are surrounding mountains in every direction. Below are residuals of last year's snow pack. Interesting red rock containing quartz crystals can be found in this area. This location is worth the substantial effort to reach it. One should plan time to remain in this area.

No evidence of further trail could be found on brief inspection. The surrounding area upward is quite brushy. One of the Stehekin rangers, who has been there, states it is possible to reach the pass beneath Mt. Logan; however, presently, it would appear to be an arduous bushwhack to surmount the brush and gain the estimated 2600' and 1 mile of linear distance to the pass. If this could be accomplished, undoubtedly the scenery would be superb.

Even if not proceeding further, the green deep grass, and blooming fireweed, lupine and asters contribute to the splendor of the area. Since this trail gets little use, a hiker can almost always obtain a sense of magnificent isolation at the trail end.

The distance from Grizzly Camp to the trail end is 4 miles. The up time lightly packed is 2 hours; down time is 1½ hours. Allow 1¼ hours to get out from Grizzly Camp to the junction with the main Bridge Creek Trail. The roundtrip time to trail end and return requires 6 hours.

There are no designated campsites beyond Grizzly Creek Camp. In general, Walker Park is the more scenic of the two campsites, but there may be a conflict between hikers and horses at this area. Grizzly Camp is for hikers only.   (August 1980)

Rainy Lake Trail

19

Map 3

Round trip: 2 miles
Elevation gain: 100'
High point: 4800'
Hiking time: 40 minutes
Difficulty: Moderately easy
USGS *Washington Pass*
Green Trails *Washington Pass*

The trailhead is on the west side of Rainy Pass, 50 yards from the North Cascades Highway, along a side road to the parking area and restrooms at the pass. The trail is blacktopped for its entire

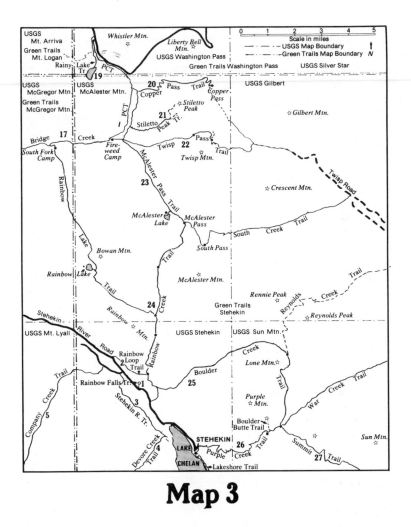

USGS
Mt. Arriva
Green Trails
Mt. Logan

Whistler Mtn. ☆

Liberty Bell Mtn. ☆

USGS Washington Pass

Green Trails Washington Pass   USGS Silver Star

Rainy Lake Tr.   PCT

19

20   Pass   Trail

Copper   *Copper Pass*

USGS Gilbert

☆ *Gilbert Mtn.*

USGS
McGregor Mtn.

USGS
McAlester Mtn.

Green Trails
McGregor Mtn.

PCT

21   *Stiletto Peak* ☆   Stiletto Peak Tr.

17   Creek   Pass

Bridge   *Fire- weed Camp*

South Fork
Camp

22   *Twisp*   Trail

Twisp Mtn.

Rainbow   Lake   Trail   McAlester Pass Trail

23

Crescent Mtn. ☆

Twisp Road

Bowan Mtn. ☆

McAlester Lake ☆   *McAlester Pass*

South   Creek   Trail

Rainbow   Lake

South Pass

McAlester Mtn. ☆

Rainbow Lake

24   Creek   Trail

Green Trails
Stehekin

Rennie Peak ☆   Reynolds   Creek   Trail

☆ *Reynolds Peak*

Stehekin -   River   Road

USGS Mt. Lyall   Rainbow   *Mtn.* ☆   Rainbow

USGS Stehekin   USGS Sun Mtn.

Rainbow
Loop
Trail   Creek

Lone Mtn. ☆

Boulder

Company   Creek   Trail

5   Rainbow Falls Tr.   1   25   *Purple Mtn.* ☆   War   Creek   Trail

3   Stehekin R. Tr.   Boulder Butte Trail   ☆

Devore Creek   Trail   4   **STEHEKIN**   **LAKE** **CHELAN**   Purple   Creek   26   Trail   Summit   ☆   *Sun Mtn.* ☆

27   Trail

Lakeshore Trail

Scale in miles
0   1   2   3   4   5
— · —   USGS Map Boundary
— · · —   Green Trails Map Boundary   *N* ↑

Map 3

1 mile distance to Rainy Lake. It is level, moderately easy, and is suitable for wheelchairs. There is adequate parking .1 mile north in the parking area.

There are scrabble trails around the lake in either direction. The lake is inviting and impressive, with a splendid waterfall descending from the snow-clad peaks to the south. Overnight camping is prohibited in the area.

The trail can also be reached without crossing the highway by the Bridge Creek/Pacific Crest Trail. It is generally open July through October. In the fall, the colorful mountain ash provide excellent color contrast with the azure blue of the lake and the gleaming white of the snowfields on the peaks above and beyond. Walking time is about 20 minutes in either direction. Water is available at the lake and at the trailhead.   (September 1979)

Copper Pass Trail

Round trip: 8.4 miles
Elevation gain: 2400'
High point: 6700'
Hiking time: 4½ hours
Difficulty: Moderately strenuous
USGS *McAlester Mtn.*
Green Trails *Stehekin*

20
Map 3

   This trail begins along the Stiletto Peak Trail. See the Stiletto Peak description for information on how to reach the trailhead. From the Stiletto Peak trailhead, continue north and follow the relatively level trail through deep woods, fording one or two minor creeks before reaching the Copper Pass trailhead in 1.2 miles. Alternatively, descend to Bridge Creek (Pacific Crest) Trail from the North Cascades Highway, one mile from the lowest point in the road between Rainy and Washington Passes, crossing State Creek enroute. Turn left (east) at a signed junction and continue east on the Copper Pass Trail; the trail to the south at .1 mile goes to the Stiletto Peak and Meadows trailhead.

   The Copper Pass Trail receives minimum maintenance, and since it is hard to locate in places, should be attempted only by experienced hikers.

   Follow the trail from the junction through timber moderately upward for .6 mile. The footpath then crosses a meadow; at the east end of the meadow, turn sharply to the left (north) and follow the trail up about 100 yards until it again goes into timber. When it emerges from the timber, it breaks out into slide alder; this is not the route. Turn back immediately and see a switchback; follow the switchbacks up through timber gaining 800' in the next .5 mile.

   A bit beyond the one mile mark, the trail levels out and stays high on the north slope of the Copper Creek Valley for the next 2 miles. It occasionally enters timber; in 1973 there was considerable windfall which had to be bypassed. Look carefully and use caution; it is not easy to find the trail in places in the meadow. 100 feet beyond the 3 mile marker, it drops slightly into a relatively level, beautiful meadow.

   The best route to Copper Pass from this point is to stay to the left (north) and then east of the trees. Pass through larch trees to reach the stream at the east end of the valley; the trail parallels the stream upward and then eventually contours across the middle portion of the meadow, reaching Copper Pass at 4.2 miles. The footpath descends steeply on the other side to join the Twisp Pass Trail, 3.1 miles away. Look for Lyall's larch beyond the 3 mile mark. Allow 2½ hours from the trailhead to Copper Pass; it takes about 2 hours to come down. The altitude gain is 2400′ from the Pacific Crest Trail junction to the pass.

Note a beautiful shallow lake below the pass. It can be reached by a cross-country traverse from the meadow below the pass. To get there, head about 10 degrees west of due south when first entering the meadow at about the 3 mile mark. There are beautiful campsites at the lake, but the lake is too shallow to support fish. The upper lake is not as pretty, and there are no suitable camping areas.

In 1973, water was available at three creeks between the trailhead and pass. Above the upper lake, there is a very interesting geologic contact zone between the golden horn granite and a much darker rock comprising the mountains to the south.

(September 1973)

Stiletto Meadows and Stiletto Peak Trail

21

Round trip: 7 miles to meadows
Elevation gain: 2300′ to meadows; 3000′ to lookout site   **Map 3**
High point: 7200′
Hiking time: 5½ hours to meadows
Difficulty: Moderately strenuous
USGS *McAlester Mtn.*
Green Trails *Stehekin*

To reach the Stiletto Meadows and Stiletto Peak trailhead from the valley, follow the Bridge Creek/Pacific Crest Trail to the Fireweed junction, about 9 miles from the Stehekin Road. Turn right (east) and follow the trail to Twisp Pass for .3 mile. Turn left (north) and follow the Stiletto Trail 1.2 miles to the trailhead. The trail continuing to the north is the access trail to Copper Pass; see that trail description for more information.

It is 5 miles from the trailhead to the site of the former Stiletto Lookout. The walking time from the junction to meadows (fully-packed) takes about 2 hours for the 3.5 mile distance. Flies and mosquitoes can be a problem in the heat of summer.

The trail is hard to find in many places after reaching the meadows. Go almost directly north, following rock cairns, to the

Stiletto Meadows

ridgecrest. Once on the ridge, the trail to the old lookout site is not difficult to follow. From the lookout area, there is a scrabble trail going eastward and down along the ridge; further cross-country descent brings one to a splendid little meadow which is an ideal campsite. Nestled under the south side of Stiletto Peak (about 1 mile east of the lookout site) is a high lake which is also a satisfactory campsite.

In the meadow, go north 100 yards, then contour east .5 mile,

picking up a small scrabble trail marked by cairns. At .4 mile,
there is a campsite with a large "20" carved on the tree. A spring
is located about 75 feet west. From almost the bottom of the trail
to this point, this is the only water, and, therefore, the only campsite. From the notch .2 mile east of this point, contour northeast
without losing altitude and drop down slightly into a small meadow
that has several streams and fair campsites. At the east portion of
this meadow, go up to a small notch with larch trees on either side.
Do not go southeast at this point in an attempt to contour around
the knoll.

The "splendid little meadow" referred to before can be reached
by this route also. The meadow is about 100 yards wide and
.4 mile long. From here, it is possible to contour around the next
ridge, drop down 200' and up a bit around another ridge to
eventually reach Twisp Pass. Also, the lake under Stiletto
Peak can be reached cross-country, using this approach.
Deer, marmots, grouse, and bear were seen in the area in 1979,
and cougar tracks were seen on the trail.

Near the old lookout site, there is one level place large enough to
pitch a two-person tent; there is no water, but it has splendid
views. The potential for a cross-country loop offers a number of
interesting options. The area is particularly impressive in the fall
when the larch turn color.

The altitude gain from the junction to the lookout site is 3000'.
Water is limited. Allow an additional hour from the meadow to the
high point on the trail. Allow 2 hours for the descent.

(August 1979)

Twisp Pass Trail

22

Round trip: 8.6 miles to pass
Elevation gain: 2200'
High point: 6066'
Hiking time: 4 hours
Difficulty: Moderately strenuous
USGS *McAlester Mtn., Gilbert*
Green Trails *Stehekin*

Map 3

This trail begins at the junction with the Pacific Crest Trail
(Bridge Creek) near Fireweed Camp. .3 mile east is the junction to
the north for the Stiletto Peak Trail and the Copper Pass Trail.
From this point, it is 2.8 miles to Dagger Lake and 3.8 miles to
Twisp Pass.

Walking time is a little more than an hour to Dagger Lake, which
is shallow, muddy and boggy. There is a table and designated
campsite by the main trail about 100 yards from the lake. It takes
another half hour to cover the additional mile to Twisp

(Twisp Pass)

Pass (6066'). The altitude gain from Fireweed to the pass is 2200'.

There are several dry campsites, far superior to Dagger Lake, in the pass area, which is the boundary between the National Forest and National Park. Follow a scrabble trail to the north for .2 mile to reach a pond; there are superb camping areas around this pond. There are some campsites to the south of the pass, but no obvious water supply in that area.

It is possible to travel cross-country between this pond and Stiletto Meadows; see the Stiletto Peak Trail for details.

From Twisp Pass, the trail descends 4.3 miles to the end of the Twisp River Road.

(Park side, July 1973; Forest side, September 1978)

McAlester Pass and Lake Trail

23

Map 3

Round trip: 20 miles from Stehekin Road;
   17 miles from North Cascades Highway
Elevation gain: 2200'
High point: 6017'
Hiking time: 2 days
Difficulty: Strenuous
USGS *McAlester Mtn.*
Green Trails *Stehekin*

From Bench Camp (see Rainbow Lake), continue up in forest 2.5 miles. Cross Rainbow Creek at this point. Bowan Campsite is near this crossing. McAlester Pass is another 2.5 miles. The last .5 mile is fairly steep. Although the trail is not too scenic, the views from the McAlester Pass area are impressive. The "pass" is really a meadow about .5 mile long with a small tarn at the southern end. It is a splendid area in which to ramble. A camping area, High Campsite, has been established at the pass itself.

McAlester Pass is 6017', 10 miles from the Stehekin Road, and 8.5 miles from the North Cascades Highway.

Near the center of the meadow is the trail junction to South Pass. It takes about 30 minutes to walk the 1.2 miles to South Pass. The trail switchbacks moderately steeply for about .3 mile, reaches a bench, and then contours without much altitude gain to the pass, which is the boundary between the Recreation Area and the National Forest. Views are spectacular, and the meadow is superb throughout this entire 1.2 mile distance.

From South Pass, it is about a 30 minute bushwhack over heather, meadow, and talus for .4 mile to two unnamed lakes nestled under McAlester Mtn. There are camping areas at both

McAlester Pass

lakes. Fish can be found in the larger lake. This faint scrabble trail is for experienced cross-country hikers only, since it is a steep traverse particularly dangerous when wet and slippery.

On the east side of South Pass, burn scars from a recent forest fire are still very evident.

It is 7 miles from South Pass to the trailhead in the Okanogan National Forest. The altitude gain is 2200'. The trail is open to motorbikes; however, they are prohibited in the Recreation Area. The trailhead begins in the South Creek Campground, 22 miles up the Twisp River Road. The approximate up-hiking time is 5 hours; down-time is 3 hours. Water and campsites are scarce along the South Creek Trail.

It is 1 mile from the trail junction at McAlester Pass to McAlester Lake, the primary established campsite in the area. Altitude loss in this mile is about 500'. Wood supplies were adequate at the lake in 1976. At the horsecamp on the southeast side of the lake, there are several tent sites, a pit toilet, and a bar for tethering horses. The hikers' camp on the north side of the lake was difficult to reach before the outlet stream was bridged in the late 1970s; this site is preferred if available. It is drier, more scenic, has no horses, and has more privacy.

Below McAlester Lake, the trail to Fireweed and the North Cascades Highway is in timber most of the way. It is 4 miles from

(McAlester Pass and Lake)

the lake to the junction with the Twisp Pass Trail. Halfway Camp is 2 miles from both the lake and trail junction. 50 yards down the trail is the Stiletto Creek spur, the quickest route northward to the North Cascades Highway. .3 mile westward is Fireweed Camp and a crossing of Bridge Creek. From this point, it is 3.3 miles via the Crest Trail to the North Cascades Highway.

The altitude loss from the lake to Fireweed is 1900'; from Fireweed to the highway, the altitude gain is 400'.

At Fireweed Camp, there are 6 to 8 campsites, tables, etc., and adequate supplies of wood and water, although the area is not particularly attractive.   (1976)

Rainbow Creek and Lake Trails

24

One way: 11 miles to Rainbow Lake; 17 miles to
    Bridge Creek

Maps 1, 3

Elevation gain: 5000' to lake (including ups and
    downs): 600' from lake to pass north of lake
High point: 5630' at lake; 6230' at unnamed pass north of lake
Hiking time: 5½ hours to lake; 3 hours from lake
    down to Bridge Creek
Difficulty: Moderately strenuous
USGS *Stehekin, McAlester Mtn., McGregor Mtn.*
Green Trails *Stehekin, McGregor Mtn.*

The trailhead is about 3 miles from Stehekin on the east side of the Stehekin-Cottonwood Camp Road. It is well-signed. The trail goes up through typically dry east-side slopes. At .2 mile, it passes a water reservoir site for the orchards below; water bottles should be filled here since there is no water from this point to the Rainbow Creek Trail crossing at 2.5 miles. (Get water from the creek nearby if the reservoir is not being used.)

From here the trail switchbacks up moderately steeply. At 1 mile, there is a fine view from the trail of Lake Chelan to the south and of the Stehekin Valley and mountains to the west. From knolls off the trail beyond this area, there are fine viewpoints and picnic spots.

At 2 miles, there is a junction with the Boulder Creek Trail. The Rainbow Creek Trail continues to the left for a few hundred yards (a scramble of .4 mile to the west from this point will bring one to the top of Rainbow Falls) and then drops down into the Rainbow Creek Valley to a bridge crossing Rainbow Creek. This is a very nice picnic spot, particularly in the spring when the entire valley is

Lake Chelan from Rainbow Creek Trail

filled with blooming dogwood. Fill water bottles here again for this is the last water for a substantial distance.

The trail then switchbacks up moderately steeply onto the side hill on the north side of the valley and follows the Rainbow Valley upward. The Rainbow Loop Trail continues northward .3 mile beyond the bridge. At 3.2 miles, there is an incredible vista from a grassy knoll, particularly impressive when the yellow balsam is blooming in the late spring. It takes about 1¼ hours to reach this viewing area. From this point, there is a fairly level traverse for 1.4 miles. There are many wildflowers along this section of the trail in the spring.

Cross Rainbow Creek on a plank bridge. 1 mile above the crossing is Bench Camp with 5 campsites in a not too scenic area. At this point, the trail forks; the left path leads to Rainbow Lake 5.5 miles further; the right trail leads to McAlester Pass.

The Rainbow Lake Trail drops down to reach Rainbow Creek, which can be forded or crossed on a crude bridge. The elevation at the ford is 3600', so 2400' have been gained since leaving the road. Drink deeply and stock up on water at this point as the next water is 2 miles, 1200', and 1½ hours away via hot, steep, dusty, dry switchbacks.

After water is reached, the trail begins to level out. 3 miles from the junction (2 hours), there is a fine view of peaks from a meadow

(Rainbow Creek and Lake)

and a good campsite nestled in the trees. Beware of mosquitoes.

On this trail, the best is saved for last! There is 600' to be gained over the last .7 mile of trail. Beautiful Sierra-type water-falls nearby lessen the pain of trudging upward again, and soon the path tops out, and drops to reach Rainbow Lake, nestled under the peaks and ridges at an altitude of 5630'. The distance covered from the Stehekin Road is 11 miles; the total altitude gained (including ups and downs) is about 5000'. Ascent time fully-packed is 5½ hours; estimated descent time is 4 hours.

The lake is very scenic, an emerald gem set in a horseshoe ring of crags and spires. There are fish in the lake. Four or five campsites are by the lake, but none of them are really comfortable for one reason or another. Firewood is available at Rainbow Lake. Mosquitoes are ubiquitous. Two lakes west of Rainbow Lake can be reached without too much difficulty by traveling cross-country. However, these lakes often retain ice much of the summer.

The trail northward climbs .9 mile from this point to an unnamed pass at 6230'. Just before the pass is reached, there is an interesting geologic transformation from granitic to much darker colored rock.

The trail drops steeply from larch forest at the top of the pass, losing 1000' in the next mile. The trail is difficult to locate in the meadow below the pass; it goes almost due north and can be found most easily by looking down when midway in the slope above the meadow, or by looking for cut-ends of avalanche-fallen trees while in the meadow. Note the splendid waterfall coming from Bowan Mountain at this point.

The trail descends through forest for a few miles and then goes through avalanche slopes with views of the surrounding mountains. The National Park boundary is 3 miles from the pass. Dan's Campsite is located midway between the pass and the Bridge Creek Trail. At 5 miles, cross Bridge Creek on a footlog. There is a 3000' loss from the pass to the junction with Bridge Creek/Pacific Crest Trail. It is 6.2 miles from the lake to Bridge Creek. There is a designated campsite (South Fork Camp at 3200') on the north side of Bridge Creek .2 mile from the Bridge Creek Trail.

From Rainbow Lake, it is a 5½ hour walk to the North Cascades Highway.

Watch carefully for rattlesnakes between the trailhead and Bench Camp.

Boulder Creek Trail

25

Round trip: 22 miles from road to junction with
  War Creek Trail

Maps 1, 3

Elevation gain: 5600'
High point: 6800'
Hiking time: allow 2 days
Difficulty: Strenuous
USGS *Stehekin, Sun Mtn.*
Green Trails *Stehekin*

The trailhead is approximately 2 miles up the Rainbow Creek Trail. The first campsite on Boulder Creek is at Rennie Creek, 4 miles from the junction, or 6 miles from the road. This trail is steep with few water sources. Near the headwaters of Boulder Creek, the trail is marked by rock cairns in the open meadow. The pathway crosses the creek and continues up the other side for 200 yards and then turns uphill and is easier to locate.

Near the ridgetop, it again crosses an open meadow marked by blazed trees and rock cairns. It continues up to the saddle in the ridge and then turns south along the flat ridgetop and is well-defined to its junction with the War Creek Trail just below War Creek Pass. At 7 miles, there is a junction with the Reynolds Creek Trail. The total trail length is 11 miles from the Stehekin Road and takes a full day up for a well-conditioned hiker, although it can be walked downward fairly comfortably in 5-6 hours. The altitude gain from the road to War Creek Pass is 5600'.

The Reynolds Creek Trail is 6.6 miles long from its start to Reynolds Pass, and it is 2.5 miles from the pass to the junction with the Boulder Creek Trail. Find the east trailhead by going up the Twisp River Road for 14 miles, crossing the War Creek Bridge, and continuing 3 miles to the trailhead. The grade is fairly easy to the pass; the trail is well-defined but gets little use.

In the near future, the Park Service plans to reroute the upper portions of the Boulder Creek Trail. The tread should be more obvious, and the upper part of the trail will terminate in the Juanita Creek area, rather than on the War Creek Trail east of War Creek Pass.

Purple Creek Trail (Purple Pass)

26

One way: 7.8 miles
Elevation gain: 5800′
High point: 6884′
Hiking time: Full day or backpack
Difficulty: Strenuous
USGS *Stehekin, Sun Mtn.*
Green Trails *Stehekin*

Maps 3, 4

(The Purples were originally homesteaders in the Stehekin area. The creek, pass, and campground are named after them. There is nothing purple-colored in the area.)

The trailhead is in back (east) of the Golden West Lodge; follow a poorly maintained road upward, past a concrete "blockhouse", to the start of the footpath. The trail switchbacks both steeply and consistently upward until Purple Pass (6884′) is reached at 7.8 miles. The trail crosses Purple Creek at 1.8 miles; in the spring, this can be a difficult crossing.

Drink deeply at this point, and fill water bottles here; water is scarce beyond this point. The next water is at Cougar Springs at 4.5 miles (unless the spring is dry) and at 4.7 miles via a scrabble trail going 200′ south to a creek. In the spring and early summer, water is available from melting snow fields near the summit, but later in the year, this is a dry, hot trail. A minimum of two water bottles is suggested. It is also desirable to start early in the day in the summer to avoid problems with overheating. It is a full day's walk for a strong hiker to reach Purple Pass and descend the additional .5 mile to the formal campsite near Juanita Lake. Lightly-packed, the walking time to the pass is about 5 hours. Add 1 to 2 hours if carrying a heavy pack. Down-time is about 3 hours.

Beyond 2.2 miles, there are a number of grassy knolls slightly off the trail where one can sit at leisure and watch the clouds and peaks reflected in the great trough of Lake Chelan. The 1500′ gain to the view areas is not too difficult, and will take the average day-hiker about 2 hours. Views improve as one goes higher; at the pass, the spectacle of the North Cascades is stirring. Larch, the only deciduous conifer, is first seen at about 6.5 miles. A larch forest graces the area between Purple and War Creek Passes.

The altitude gain is 5800′ to the pass. There are reasonable amounts of wood near Juanita Camp. Wildflowers are impressive in June. Deer are commonly seen on the trail, as well as an occasional bear. Carry an ice ax during ascents in May and June, since snow can be anticipated on the last 1 to 2 miles of the trail during these months. (See Summit Trail description for additional information about the Boulder Butte and Juanita Lake areas.)

(July 1979)

Lake Chelan from Purple Pass Trail

Summit Trail

27

One way: 30 miles to Purple Pass
Elevation gain: 8500' with ups and downs
High point: 7400'
Hiking time: 3 to 4 days
Difficulty: Moderately strenuous
USGS *Sun Mtn., Oval Peak 7½ ' or Buttermilk Butte 15 ',*
   Prince Creek, Martin Peak
Green Trails *Stehekin, Buttermilk Butte, Prince Creek*

Maps 3, 4

From Purple Pass, the trail drops down .7 mile to reach Juanita
Camp. At .2 mile is the junction with the Boulder Butte Trail. This
side trail to the site of an old demolished lookout is .5 mile long and
gains 450'. Enjoy an incredible 360 degree panorama from an
elevation of 7372'. This is one of the most beautiful places in the
North Cascades. This side trip must not be missed under any
circumstances. Ideally, the area should be visited in the late afternoon, at sunset, and the following morning in order to appreciate
different lighting at these three times of day.

Juanita Camp is pleasant except for the mosquitoes and has
widely scattered camping areas over a distance of .3 mile. Juanita
Lake is shallow and could be considered simply a high tarn; it does
not contain fish. Walk above Juanita Lake to the junction with the
Summit Trail and a bit above that to War Creek Pass.

From this junction, the Summit Trail proceeds southeast, losing
500' in the first mile. Then it switchbacks up to reach a high, flat
ridge at about the 3 mile mark. This ridge is the boundary
between the Wenatchee National Forest and the Lake Chelan
National Recreation Area. It is a very scenic place with many good
campsites. There was considerable snow in July available as a
water source, but it is anticipated it would be a dry camp later in
the year. The altitude gain to this ridge is 1500' from the low point
on the trail.

The path runs along the ridge for about .3 mile and then
descends. In .5 mile, the 26 mile marker is passed. Less than
1 mile further is Camp Comfort, a reasonably pleasant campsite
with good access to water, but without views. Continue down.
Near the low point between the 23 and 24 mile markers 'is the
junction with the North Fork of the Fish Creek Trail. This junction
was neither signed nor obvious in 1979. 1.5 miles further, and
uphill, is the junction with the Eagle Pass Trail. It is 1 mile to the
pass, and an additional 7.5 miles from the pass to the roadhead of
the Eagle Creek Trail.

From here the Summit Trail goes up steeply to reach a scenic
pass at the 21 mile marker (miles are measured from the south,
rather than from the north). Drop 1 mile into a meadow with a

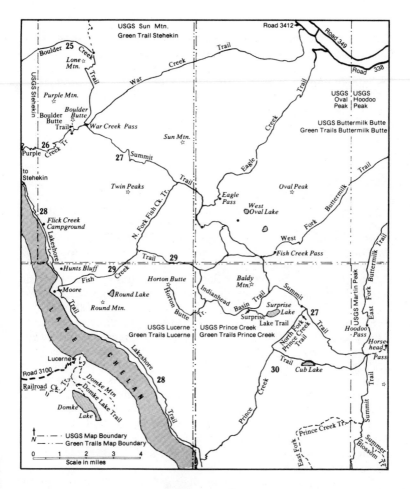

Map 4

splendid campsite 150 feet beyond the 20 mile marker. At the campsite is the junction with the Horseshoe Spur Trail; the (east) Fish Creek Trail is 1.5 miles, and Lake Chelan is 10 miles to the west. The National Recreation Area boundary is 6.5 miles north. Water is available from a small creek right next to the campsite. Cross-country exploration of the surrounding meadow is quite feasible.

Immediately past the camp, the trail ascends sharply and gains

(Summit Trail)

200'. From here, it contours gradually up to the 18 mile marker, where there is a junction. From this point, Fish Creek Pass is .5 mile east on the West Fork Buttermilk Trail #411. There are several fair campsites both north and south of the 18 mile marker. South of the junction, no tread can be found in the meadow for about 150 yards. Contour south through the meadow to pick it up. From this point, the trail goes up steeply and crosses over a high pass beneath Star Peak; there are good views in all directions from the pass.

The trail again goes down. In 1 mile, the junction with the Surprise Lake Trail is reached. The trail is difficult to locate for 200 feet at the junction, and caution is necessary to be sure the right path is taken here. At the junction, there is a nice campsite with a log table, but no view. The Summit Trail continues down from the junction to reach the North Fork Shelter near the 15 mile marker; the shelter is in good condition with water closeby, but it is not located in a scenic area.

Surprise Lake, Indianhead Basin, Horton Butte, and the Fish Creek Trails can be reached by turning right (southwest) at the junction noted before. It is 1.5 miles with 800' gain to the start of the Surprise Lake way trail; from here, it is 1.1 miles to the lake. The last .5 mile is steep and rocky. There is a campsite, primarily for trail bikers, just before the steep descent to the lake. Hikers and horsemen will prefer the developed campsites at the lake itself. Continuing on through Indianhead Basin, it is 2.8 miles to the junction with the Horton Butte Trail; from here, it is 2.5 miles to the lookout site, and about 2 miles to the Fish Creek Trail.

.5 mile beyond the North Fork Shelter (on the Summit Trail), the junction with the North Fork of the Prince Creek Trail is reached. From here, the main Prince Creek Trail is 2 miles, and Lake Chelan is 9 miles to the west.

The trail goes up from this point, reaching a scenic pass with great views in all directions at about the 12 mile marker. Contouring along the ridge .5 mile further, there is a splendid view down Prince Creek. .9 mile beyond is the junction with the trail to Hoodoo Pass, 1 mile to the east. South .2 mile is the junction with the Boiling Lake Trail to the east and the Middle Fork of Prince Creek Trail to the southwest.

There is a good campsite 100 feet north of the junction. There are even nicer campsites at Boiling Lake, which is .5 mile, 500' higher, and 20 minutes of hiking time away! From Boiling Lake, Horsehead Pass is .5 mile to the east (see Eagle Lake Trail information). Via the Middle Fork of Prince Creek Trail, Cub Lake is 2.5 miles to the west, and Lake Chelan is 11 miles away. A new

Juanita Lake from Boulder Butte

trail connecting Boiling and Cub Lakes is scheduled to be constructed in 1980.

It is possible to continue southeast from Boiling Lake to the primitive road near South Navarre Mountain, or to take the Summer Blossom cut-off (for hikers only) and reach the primitive road near Falls Creek. The latter option is preferred, both because it avoids trail machines and because the access road is of better quality, although still a difficult drive.

From the Boiling Lake/Summit Trail junction, it is 1.2 miles to water and a campsite. Proceeding south 1.6 miles, the junction with the East Fork of the Prince Creek Trail is reached. From this point, it is 3 miles to Prince Creek, and 8 miles to Uno Peak. This way trail was difficult to locate, but signed "closed to cycles". The junction is in an enjoyable meadow with many campsites.

Just south of the meadow, the trail switchbacks up a ridge; the 7 mile marker is on the switchbacks. On the ridge, 6.7 miles from the South Navarre Campground, is the junction with the Summer Blossom Trail. This trail is signed only with a diagramatic sign prohibiting cycle use (a drawing of a cycle with a red slash through it). The trail turns left at the ridge; the more obvious Summit Trail continues to the right, dropping down somewhat into the forest. Since the Summit Trail to South Navarre Campground is open to trail machines and since the trailhead is more difficult for vehicle

(Summit Trail)

access, the Summer Blossom Trail is recommended for hikers.

From the junction, the Summer Blossom Trail goes southeast. A way trail is passed after .5 mile. From here, the trail drops down, losing about 400' to reach a campsite of fair quality with good water in the meadow immediately below the ridge. The trail then goes up, and about 3 miles from the Summer Blossom trailhead, reaches a crest with impressive views. Then it descends somewhat less steeply. There is no water from the campsite described to .5 mile from the road. There is parking for several cars across the road from the trailhead, and water is available from Falls Creek 50 yards away.

To reach the Summer Blossom trailhead by car, drive north from Chelan on U. S. 97 and turn left at Pateros, 19 miles from the Chelan Bridge. Continue on State Highway 153 for 16.8 miles and turn left immediately before a bridge over the Methow River. .8 mile beyond, turn left onto the Gold Creek Road #3109. After an additional mile, turn left on Road #3107, and remain on this road for 5.5 more miles. Turn right at that junction, and follow Road #3107 an additional 8.3 miles to the crest between the Okanogan and Chelan drainages. Turn right and follow this road north an additional 8.4 miles to the trailhead. The road is difficult, exposed, rough, and dusty, and for experienced back country drivers only.

Although the Summer Blossom Trail is signed as 8.1 km (5 miles), the author estimates after walking it that it was about 6 miles in length.   (July 1979)

Accesses From Twisp Drainage to Summit Trail

East-side accesses to the Summit Trail and the crest between the Stehekin and Twisp drainages include the West Fork Buttermilk Trail #411, East Fork Buttermilk Trail #420, and the Eagle Lake Trail #431.

WEST FORK BUTTERMILK TRAIL

The West Fork Trail is 9.5 miles to the pass with an approximate hiking time of 5 hours. The trail disappears in spots when crossing meadows, campsites are limited, and there are substantial boggy areas. The altitude gain is from 3600' to 7500'. This trail is not recommended.

EAST FORK BUTTERMILK TRAIL

The East Fork Buttermilk Trail is considerably shorter at 6.5 miles, starts higher at 4700', and has a shorter hiking time of about 4 hours. To reach the trailhead, take the Twisp River Road 11 miles, turn left, cross the river, and proceed 7 miles and turn right on the Buttermilk Butte Road for 2.2 miles to a sharp turn where there are parking places for several cars. (Buttermilk Butte is 2 miles beyond with spectacular views in all directions.) The first 2 miles are level; the second 2 miles are steeper, and the last section of the trail is boggy, changing to steep and rocky near the summit. From Hoodoo Pass, it is a short mile to the junction with the Summit Trail and the trail to Cub Lake along the Middle Fork of Prince Creek.

EAGLE LAKE TRAIL #431

Perhaps the most scenic and enjoyable east-side access route is the Eagle Lake Trail. The trailhead is reached from either Black Pine Lake on the north, or State Highway 153 on the south. Turn off the Gold Creek Road at Crater Creek Camp and drive almost to the road end, where there is parking for 6 or 7 cars at the trailhead and for several more cars at the road end .1 mile to the north.

From this point, it is 7 miles to Horsehead Pass. The trail goes up and contours along the cliffside, crossing Crater Creek at .7 mile. At 1 mile, there is a view. At exactly 2 miles is the Martin Creek Trail junction. At 2.5 miles, there is a campsite on the right with water available from a small spring 100' further up the trail.

At 6 miles (3 hours) is Middle Eagle Lake with a number of boggy but reasonably satisfactory campsites. Trails at or near this point go to both upper and lower Eagle Lakes. From Middle Eagle Lake, it is 1 mile and 500' higher to Horsehead Pass. From the pass, it is .5 mile to Boiling Lake, and 1 mile to the junction with the Summit Trail.

There is a splendid campsite 100 yards beyond Middle Eagle Lake just prior to crossing the small outlet creek. The up-time to the pass lightly-packed is 3¼ hours; down-time is 2½ hours. Altitude gain is 2500'. There are fish in all three lakes. (July 1979)

WAR CREEK

The War Creek Trail is 9.3 miles long with an approximate upward hiking time of 5 hours. To reach the trailhead, drive 14.7 miles from Twisp on the Twisp River Road, turn south, and cross the Twisp River. Turn right in .5 mile, and follow the road on the south side of the river about 4 miles; turn left and drive 2.2 miles to the trailhead.

The ascent is gradual for about the first 8 miles, but the path steepens as it climbs the last 1.3 miles to War Creek Pass. The

(Summit Trail — War Creek access)

altitude gain on the War Creek Trail is from 3120' to 6800'. The War Creek Trail joins the Summit Trail just east of Juanita Lake.

OTHER TRAILS

There is intermittent trail from the Horseshoe Spur junction up to Tuckaway Lake. A scrabble trail leads from near the lake over Oval Pass to connect with the Oval Lakes Trail; see Fish Creek Trail for further details.

Lakeshore Trail

28

One way: 17 miles
Elevation gain: 3000' total including ups and downs
High point: 2000'
Hiking time: 2 days
Difficulty: Moderate
USGS *Stehekin, Sun Mtn., Lucerne, Prince Creek*
Green Trails *Stehekin, Lucerne, Prince Creek*

Maps 3, 4

The boat disembarcation point is .2 mile north of the mouth of Prince Creek. Walk southeast to the creek and cross it on a narrow but serviceable log bridge. There are a number of satisfactory campsites near the creek mouth. From the Prince Creek Trail junction, it is 6 miles to Meadow Creek, 11 miles to Fish Creek, and 17 miles to Stehekin. Less than 1 mile to the south is the official Prince Creek Campground.

In the first mile to the north, the trail gains 500' and reaches a good viewpoint at the 16 mile point. There is another corner with a good view .5 mile beyond. Just before the 14 mile marker, there is another substantial altitude gain. Shortly thereafter, Rex Creek is forded. Just beyond Rex Creek, there is a trail shelter in good condition, but in an unappealing location without any views. At about the 11 mile mark, cross Cascade Creek. There is one poor campsite near the creek.

At 10 miles is Meadow Creek where there is another unattractive shelter (in good condition) in the deep forest. If you walk down toward the lake, you will reach private property, liberally marked with no trespassing signs. .7 mile beyond the shelter (.2 mile north of the 10 mile sign), leave the trail to the left, lose about 150' of elevation and find two lovely campsites in the ponderosa pines just above the lake. A short scramble over Class 2 rock gives access to the lakeshore for bathing, drinking, and cooking water. There are great views from this point to the north

Lake Chelan from Lakeshore Trail

and south. Directly across the lake from this campsite is Lucerne. There are no other satisfactory camping areas from here to Moore Point, 3 miles to the north.

The first 7.7 miles is hot, even in the spring, has lots of ups and downs, and is fatiguing. Watch for ticks, and, more importantly, look out for rattlesnakes.

At 9.8 miles, the trail loses several hundred feet of elevation as it switchbacks down to a pasture east of Moore. .4 mile further, the Fish Creek Bridge is reached. At this point, there are two important junctions; it is .5 mile downstream to the lakeshore and the established campground at Moore Point. Lilacs and iris, relics of the old Moore Hotel, still bloom in season near the campground. Upstream, the Fish Creek Trail leads to the high meadows. See the Fish Creek Trail description. .2 mile beyond the bridge is the junction of several roads. Here is a newly roofed shelter with water nearby from a creek, but again, no view.

The route now gains 1000' in the next 1.5 miles to reach the high point on Hunt's Bluff at the 5 mile marker. This is an excellent place to eat lunch.

After descending the bluff, cross Hunt's Creek. In an additional mile, the boundary of the Lake Chelan National Recreation Area is reached, and shortly beyond this point is the Flick Creek Shelter, located on the lakeshore with a delightful view to the south. There

Looking uplake toward Stehekin from Hunt's Bluff

(Lakeshore Trail)

are very few flat spots around the shelter; this area probably could not handle more than 5 or 6 overnight campers simultaneously, and is the only designated campsite between the National Recreation Area boundary and Stehekin.

Cross pretty Flick Creek 1 mile north of the shelter. .9 mile beyond is Fourmile Creek; 1.3 miles after that is Hazard Creek. It is another .7 mile beyond Hazard Creek to the south end of Stehekin.

Although called the Lakeshore Trail, the trail seldom runs along the lakeshore. Most of the time it is 200' to 500' above the lake, making it difficult to reach the lake for water, campsites, etc. The elevation gain in the entire 17 miles is 3000'. Water is available from the creeks mentioned, or at the lake if reachable. Good campsites are scarce. Perhaps 5 of the 17 miles are in forest, without views, but the other 12 miles are relatively open and do give panoramas up, down, and across the lake. This hike is best done in the spring and fall, and should be avoided during the heat of the summer.

High boots and long pants are recommended, since almost everyone walking this 17 mile distance will meet at least one rattlesnake. Check carefully when reaching Stehekin to remove any ticks that have been accumulated during the trip.

(May 1979)

Fish Creek Trail

29

One way (to Summit Trail): North Fork, 6.6 miles
  East Fork, 9.7 miles   **Map 4**
Elevation gain: North Fork, 4300'; East Fork, 5300'
High point: North Fork, 5500'; East Fork, 6500'
Hiking Time: 1 day
Difficulty: Strenuous
USGS *Buttermilk Butte, Lucerne, Prince Creek, Sun Mtn.*
Green Trails *Lucerne, Stehekin, Prince Creek, Buttermilk Butte*

The lower trailhead is at the shelter .2 mile north of the bridge over Fish Creek on the Lakeshore Trail at 1200'. The main trail and the North Fork Trail #1248A are heavily used by horses, and the resultant rubble (dust when dry; mud when wet) create unpleasant walking conditions for the hiker. The map shows a junction with the unmaintained trail to Round Lake at 1.7 miles. However, no trail sign or obvious trail can be seen at this location.

At 3.3 miles is the North Fork Shelter. The roof is in poor condition and is not waterproof. There is a table in the shelter. Multiple satisfactory tent sites are in the area immediately surrounding the deteriorating cabin. Water can be obtained from Fish Creek, which cascades downward 50' in front of the shelter. .4 mile further, the trail divides. The North Fork Trail goes up through woods, crosses another creek at about 4.7 miles and joins the Summit Trail at 5500', 6.6 miles from the trailhead.

The East Fork Trail crosses the North Fork of the creek at this point. This crossing can be hazardous during the spring high water runoff. It is 6 miles from this point to the Summit Trail by this route; however, this trail has relatively little horse use and is in much better condition. After the crossing, the trail switchbacks up fairly steeply for .5 mile; then the ascent is more gradual. The trail crosses intermittent open areas with flowers and vistas.

In 3 miles, the hiker must ford the East Fork of the creek; a crude ladder was in place here in 1980. The first campsite since the North Fork Shelter is adjacent to the ford; several additional camping areas are located on a bench 50' above the ford on the north side of the creek; there is no obvious way-trail to these additional tent sites. This crossing can also be hazardous in times of high runoff.

At 6.5 miles is the signed trail junction with Indianhead Basin. This trail also leads to Surprise Lake and Horton Butte. (See description on page 104.) .8 mile further up the East Fork Trail, there is a poor campsite located underneath poles arranged in the shape of an A frame. Several smaller creeks must also be

(Fish Creek)

crossed.   .4 mile beyond this campsite, there is 200' of bog. Above the bog .2 mile is the junction with the unmaintained Horseshoe Spur Trail. The main East Fork Trail continues to join the Summit Trail at 6500', 2 miles from the junction.

The Horseshoe Spur Trail is the shortest route to Tuckaway Lake and Oval Pass. This 1.5 mile bypass is not difficult to follow, except in the upper meadow where no tread is visible, but bypassing windfall is time consuming and unpleasant. Watch for double blazes on trees and cut log ends if the tread is vague or non-existant. There is an excellent campsite at the junction of the Horseshoe Spur with the Summit Trail. From this junction, a way trail goes upward through gorgeous meadow, gaining 500' in .7 mile to reach Tuckaway Lake, nestled near the crest of the mountains. There is a lovely campsite with a log table at the lake. There also are many fish in the lake. Splendid meadows are reached 1 mile up the Horseshoe Spur Trail, and continue to the Chelan crest. From Tuckaway Lake, it is possible to follow an easily found scrabble trail to Oval Pass; drop down on the east side of the crest to reach the scenic Oval Lakes with excellent campsites.

The Indianhead Basin Trail switchbacks steeply. Water can be obtained at 2 places along the trail. It takes 50 minutes to reach the first campsite in a scenic but buggy meadow. Water is available from a small stream 100' to the east. Here is also a junction with a way trail signed "Dead end 1.5 miles"; the main trail continues to Surprise Lake 2.5 miles away.

The side trail was thought to be the Horton Butte Trail. Tread was vague in places, but both old and new blazes helped with route-finding. At .9 mile, this trail reached a crest, and an unsigned junction. One trail descends steeply to the west. The second trail, which is less apparent but recently blazed and maintained, leads south .3 mile. At that point, it is a steep 100 yard scrabble to the top of a ridge. Walk .2 mile to the southeast for a viewpoint of Lucerne and Lake Chelan lying in its deep, glacier-carved trough below. Evidence that this was the site of the Horton Butte Lookout could not be found. Another way trail from the ridge had been recently maintained and led down along the bluff to the west for at least .5 mile.

(Later information from the Forest Service indicates: The trail descending steeply to the west is indeed the Horton Butte Trail. It ascends the ridge to the west; the lookout site can be reached by a short ridge walk to the north. The distance from the crest is about 1.6 miles. The way trail along the ridge is the upper end of the Blue Jay Trail. This footpath ultimately terminates at or near the

Meadow Creek Shelter on the Lakeshore Trail; it receives very limited maintenance.)

The view from Horton Butte down toward Lake Chelan is reported to be elegant.

The entire Fish Creek drainage is closed to trail machines, although they are allowed within .5 mile of Surprise Lake if coming from the south via the Summit Trail.

The higher portions of this trail are generally snowfree in early July. Watch for rattlesnakes at lower altitudes.

Prince Creek Trail

30

One way: 9 miles to Summit Trail via North Fork;
    11 miles via Middle Fork   **Map 4**
Elevation gain: 4500' via North Fork; 5500' via Middle Fork
High point: 5600' (North Fork); 6600' (Middle Fork)
Hiking time: 1½ days
Difficulty: Moderately strenuous
USGS *Prince Creek, Martin Peak*
Green Trails *Prince Creek*

The trailhead is .1 mile northwest of Prince Creek and .1 mile southeast of the boat debarking point. There are a number of satisfactory campsites in the immediate area. From this point it is 7 miles to the Prince Creek Trail North Fork junction, 8 miles to Cub Lake, 9 miles to the Summit Trail (via the North Fork), and 11 miles to the Summit Trail via the Middle Fork.

The altitude gain via the North Fork is 4500'; via the Middle Fork, the gain is 5500'. Water is scarce the first 8 miles. The trail stays on the north side of the creek for 4 miles. It then crosses Prince Creek and remains on the south side of the creek until it crosses the Middle Fork just below the trail junction between the forks. The crossing elevations are 2715' and 4200'. Water is available at only these two points. Both crossings may be hazardous during the high water runoff in the spring and early summer.

There are campsites at the 4 and 6 mile points. There is an established campsite with picnic tables, fire grates, and toilets at Cub Lake. The trail from Cub Lake to the Summit Trail is scheduled for reconstruction in 1980. There is usually good fishing at Cub Lake. Watch carefully for rattlesnakes on the lower portions of this trail.

The North Fork Trail is often brushy. There are several undeveloped campsites in the 2 mile length of this trail. This trail is closed to trail machines.

Most hikers will take 1½ days to reach the high country by

either Prince Creek Trail route, although strong experienced hikers can do it in one long day. Down-time is comfortably less and can easily be done in 5 hours from the north and 6 hours from the south.

Index to Topographic Maps

USGS Maps
(All 7½ ', unless indicated otherwise)

a	Diablo Dam	s	Slate Peak
b	Ross Dam	t	Robinson Mtn.
c	Eldorado Peak	u	Washington Pass
d	Forbidden Peak	v	Silver Star Mtn.
e	Sonny Boy Lakes	w	McAlester Mtn.
f	Cascade Pass	x	Gilbert
g	Downey Mtn.	y	Stehekin
h	Dome Peak	z	Sun Mtn.
i	Glacier Peak - 15'	aa	Lucerne - 15'
j	Crater Mtn.	bb	Mazama - 15'
k	Azurite Peak		
l	Mt. Logan	CC	Buttermilk Butte — 15'
m	Mt. Arriva	cc	Midnight Mtn.
		dd	Thompson Ridge
n	Goode Mtn.	ee	Oval Peak
o	McGregor Mtn.	ff	Hoodoo Peak
p	Agnes Mtn.		
q	Mt. Lyall	gg	Prince Creek
		hh	Martin Peak
r	Holden - 15'	ii	Big Goat Mtn.
		jj	South Navarre Peak

Index to Topographic Maps

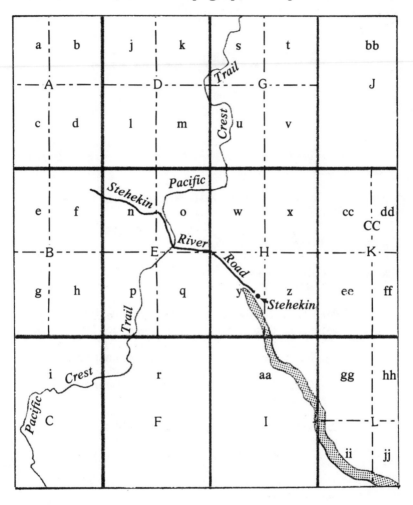

Green Trails Maps (All 15′)

A	Diablo Dam	G	Washington Pass
B	Cascade Pass	H	Stehekin
C	Glacier Peak	I	Lucerne
D	Mt. Logan	J	Mazama
E	McGregor Mtn.	K	Buttermilk Butte
F	Holden	L	Prince Creek

Bibliography

Darvill's Guide to the North Cascades National Park and Associated Areas, Volumes I and II by Dr. Fred Darvill, 1972, 1975 (revised)

Stehekin - A Wilderness Journey into the North Cascades, by W. A.Bake, National Park Service, 1977

Exploring Washington by H. M. Majors, 1975

Glaciation of the Chelan Trough by P. A. Barker, Washington State University

Lake Chelan: Bottom Topography by J. T. Whetter, University of Washington, Department of Oceanography

North Cascades National Park, Ross Lake National Recreation Area, and Lake Chelan National Recreation Area: History Basic Data by Erwin Thompson, National Park Service, 1970

Lake Chelan in the 1890s by Robert Byrd, World Publishing Co., Wenatchee, 1972

Index

Acknowledgments

Illustrations and map of rivers and creeks of Stehekin Valley:
Marjorie Domenowske

History: Dr. A. D. Martinson, Pacific Lutheran University,
Tacoma, Washington.

Photographs:
Field Hotel, courtesy of Chelan Historial Society, Chelan, WA
Magic Mountain, by Lee Mann
All other photos, by Fred Darvill, Jr.

Data on Lookouts: S.A. Beeson and Ray Kresek

Sketch of Stehekin Landing: courtesy of Gary Gibson of the North
Cascades Lodge

Short sections of this book were originally published in Darvill's
Guide to the North Cascades National Park and Associated Areas
and are printed by permission of Dr. Fred Darvill. Material written
by contributing authors in the above booklet has been utilized in
part in this publication. The author expresses gratitude for the
contribution of William Rivord in the section on botany, and
to Dolly Connelly for insights into North Cascade history.

Overall review of manuscript: Alan Eliason, Naturalist, North
Cascades National Park.

The author, overlooking Stehekin Valley from McGregor Mountain

About the Author

Dr. Fred Darvill began his love affair with the wilderness world after completing his postgraduate training in internal medicine in 1956. He has spent substantial time over the past 24 years searching for challenges and beauty throughout the world. He has seen many of the great peaks of the world, including McKinley, Aconcagua, Kilimanjaro, and Everest; he has climbed and hiked in Asia, Africa, New Zealand, Australia and South America, as well as North America. However, he always returns to the North Cascades with the sense that these are the most splendid valleys and peaks to be found anywhere. He feels the Stehekin Valley is a unique and very special place, which he would like to share with the readers of this book.

Other books written by Dr. Darvill include *Mountaineering Medicine - A Wilderness Medical Guide* and several guides to the North Cascades, of which *North Cascades Highway Guide* and *North Cascades National Park Guide (West Section)* are still in print. He was a contributor to *Medicine for Mountaineering* published by The Mountaineers. He co-authored *Winter Walks and Summer Strolls,* a guide to lowland trails in northwest Washington, with Louise Marshall. He has written two privately published books of poetry. His photograph of his daughter on the Cascade Pass Trail won the grand prize in the American Museum of Natural History photography contest in 1977. He is currently writing a book on the North Cascades for the Sierra Club.

Other Books by Dr. Darvill

Mountaineering Medicine (A Wilderness Medical Guide)
Designed to be carried in a pack with a first aid kit. Its 60 pages detail diagnosis and treatment for all reasonably common illnesses and injuries likely to occur in the wilderness. Published by the Skagit Mountain Rescue Unit, P.O. Box 2, Mount Vernon, WA 98273.   9th edition, 1980 $1.95
"I would like to compliment you on your booklet, Mountaineering Medicine, *which is easily the most compact and comprehensive that I have seen."*

> —*Dr. Charles Houston, director of the Mt. Logan High Altitude Experiment Station*

Guide to the North Cascades National Park and Associated Areas
PART I—General information about the Park and related areas. Sections on birds, animals, plants, geology and history. Photographs and map. Detailed guide to 89 trails west of the Cascade Crest between Stevens Pass and Manning Park. $1.75

●

PART II—Guide to 50 trails on or east of the Cascade Crest. (now out of print). A substantial amount of material in Part II is incorporated into *STEHEKIN: The Enchanted Valley.*
Information previously presented in Parts I and II will be included in a Sierra Club Tote-Book Guide to the North Cascades, which is scheduled for publication in Spring of 1982.

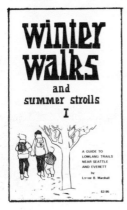

Winter Walks and Summer Strolls with Louise Marshall
This book describes almost all the commonly accessible lowland trails in the four northwestern counties of Washington State. $2.95

North Cascades Highway Guide
Contents include map of the highway, a guide to all points of interest, and sections on history, geology, botany, ornithology, zoology and trails of the area. $1.00

**Darvill Outdoor Publications
1819 Hickox Road
Mount Vernon, WA 98273**

(Add 50¢ per order for postage. Washington State residents add 5.3% sales tax.)